**Teaching people with
severe learning difficulties**

EDY

Trainee workbook

Second edition

Judith McBrien, Peter Farrell and Tom Foxen

Manchester University Press

Manchester and New York

Distributed exclusively in the USA and Canada by St. Martin's Press

CONTENTS

Page

Foreword: Peter Mittler   iii
Preface   vii
Acknowledgements   ix

Introduction   1

PHASE I: The EDY Training Course   9

Introduction to the practical work for all units   11

Unit 1: Antecedents and Setting Conditions   13

Unit 2: Planning Individual Teaching Sessions   31

Unit 3: Using Rewards   47

Unit 4: Prompting   73

Unit 5: Task Analysis   87

Unit 6: Shaping   111

Unit 7: Imitation   133

Unit 8: Putting It All Together   145

PHASE II: Applying EDY in Context   157

A   Planning Individual Teaching Programmes   161

B   Room Management   175

Bibliography   181

Answers to study questions for each unit on Phase I   185

Appendix I   Spare Recording Sheets
Appendix II   Evaluation Materials (for the course instructor)

Note on terminology

Throughout the *Trainee workbook* and *Instructor's handbook* we have used the term Severe Learning Difficulty rather than Learning Disabilty. We acknowledge that, at the time of writing, the term Learning Disability has been adopted in adult settings in the United Kingdom. For children the term Severe Learning Difficulty is used and there are no immediate moves to change this. As the majority of EDY users work in schools, we have decided to use the term Severe Learning Difficulty throughout. However, the materials are specifically designed to meet the training needs of staff who work with *all* people who have severe learning difficulties/disabilities.

FOREWORD

PETER MITTLER: Professor of Special Education and Dean of the Faculty of Education, University of Manchester.

This revised edition of the EDY (Education of Developmentally Young) course on behavioural methods of teaching children and adults with severe learning difficulties is based not only on many years of research and experience with the course but also takes account of the major developments in professional practice which have taken placed since the course was first developed in the 1970s. What are these changes and what significance do they have for a new edition of EDY?

Firstly, teachers and other professionals have become much more proficient in the use of behavioural methods, due in part at least to the dissemination of EDY and similar training initiatives. Proficiency here involves not merely the correct use of the training techniques but their adaptation to the day to day realities of practice and the needs of individual learners. This process has been so successful that it is said that some practitioners or services are 'beyond behavioural methods'. This may mean that behavioural methods are truly integrated into the ordinary teaching activities in the classroom or the workplace and are not as clearly in evidence as they might have been some years ago. But although there are now fewer examples of edible rewards or loud shouts of "good boy/girl", both at one time wrongly regarded as the hallmark of a behavioural approach, staff are almost automatically practising many of the essential elements of a behavioural approach - e.g. setting clear and attainable goals, task analysis, prompting, shaping and consistent use of appropriate rewards. Furthermore, they have become more proficient in incorporating behavioural methods into group work, again partly through the incorporation of principles of room management, now integrated into Phase 2 of the present revision.

If the 1970s were the decade of behavioural methods, the 1980s saw the development of a great deal of school-based curricular development. Staff devoted many hours to working out a school curriculum which was then adapted to the needs of individual students. Behavioural methods were merely a means to the end of meeting the needs of the individual.

The advent of the national curriculum for all school-age pupils between 5 and 16 years of age throws all these developments into sharp relief. All schools for children with severe learning difficulties are in the process of a radical review of the whole curriculum - i.e. "the sum of all the experiences provided by a school for its students" (HMI 1985). This now includes the school's already established curriculum, the pupil's individual educational plan, the national curriculum and the whole curriculum: no mean feat in eleven years of compulsory education. Nevertheless, many schools are energetically tackling this task, fuelled by determination to avoid the exclusion of their children from the entitlement to a "broad, balanced and relevant curriculum" which is theirs by law.

Official pronouncements from the Department of Education and Science, HMI, the National Curriculum Council and the School Examinations and Assessment Council all emphasise that the National Curriculum is for all pupils and that there is to be a minimum of exceptions, modifications and disapplications. Whether these intentions are realised depends to a large extent on the quality of the support given to teachers and other professionals working with pupils with severe learning difficulties. So far, there is evidence that this is the most active of all sectors of special needs provision. Published materials intended to provide guidance and examples of good practice and INSET materials have been provided by Manchester Teacher Fellows (Fagg, Aherne, Skelton and Thornber 1990; Fagg and Skelton 1990; Aherne and Thornber 1990a, 1990b; Ackerman and Mount 1991; Mount and Ackerman 1991), by the National Curriculum Development Team based at the Cambridge Institute of Education (NCC 1991) and in a very helpful book edited by Ashdown, Carpenter and Bovair (1991).

Developments in the provision of appropriate services for school leavers and adults with learning difficulties have been uneven and patchy and have not on the whole matched the quality of provision or staffing levels available to children of school age. On the positive side, there has been a substantial reduction in the number of adults living in long stay residential hospitals and some success in providing access to community services, particularly the use of ordinary housing, with levels of support matched to the needs of the individuals living in the house. There has also been a modest increase in the number of people who have secured employment. But there are still some 60,000 people with learning difficulties attending segregated day centres, most of which are underfunded and understaffed, with very limited access to appropriate training opportunities. The quality of life and services for people with learning difficulties living in the community is sometimes very poor; Flynn's (1988) research suggests that some of them are severely victimised by neighbours and lead lives characterised by loneliness and poverty.

The aspiration of service planners and providers to provide a life style "as close to normal as possible" is supported by the goals of normalisation and the principle of aiming for a valued social role for people with learning difficulties (Wolfensberger 1983). These principles have been immensely influential but sometimes misunderstood and misapplied. In a recent chapter on ethical aspects of behaviour analysis in relation to normalisation (Kiernan 1991) argues convincingly that measures taken to help people with learning difficulties to develop competence and autonomy need not be inconsistent with principles of normalisation. Similarly, the authors of the present edition of EDY, see EDY Instructor's Handbook, address some of the major criticisms of behavioural methods which have been advanced in recent years and show that at least some of these are based on a misunderstanding of the behavioural approach to teaching. For example, there is no reason in principle why the use of such approaches automatically denies choices to individuals or prevents them from having a say in determining teaching priorities or methods. The fact that such choices have not always been available reflects a misapplication of behavioural methods rather than a fundamental criticism of the methods themselves. Similarly, there is no necessary conflict between the appropriate use of behavioural methods and the current emphasis on interactive teaching.

It is true that the advent of behavioural methods in the late 60s and early 70s generated a misplaced enthusiasm and a conviction by a few individuals that such methods should underpin each and every aspect of the work of an organisation. Major advances have taken placed in the development of both the theory and practice of behavioural methods (e.g. Remington 1991) such that many professionals now use such methods only in a context where they seem appropriate and potentially able to help an individual to acquire certain skills and competencies.

The time has certainly come to place such approaches in a more humanitarian and a more caring context. On the other hand, it can be argued that all professionals should have a working knowledge both of the theory and practice of behavioural methods, in order to make an informed judgment of when and how they can be used to best advantage. Behavioural methods are one of a number of intervention strategies which can be used by practitioners and parents and in no way demand that other methods should be abandoned or considered less valuable. As they have such an important role to play in helping people to learn and acquire new skills, all staff should have opportunities to become proficient in their use.

PREFACE

EDY (Education of the Developmentally Young) is a training course for staff and parents who live and work with people who have severe learning difficulties (children and adults). It provides training in the application of behavioural methods when teaching new skills. The importance of behavioural methods has been recognised for many years, although initiatives to train staff in how to use these techniques were slow to follow. EDY is one of several training courses that were developed in the late 1970s and has had considerable impact since it was first published, (Foxen and McBrien, 1981; McBrien and Foxen, 1981).

The original EDY course was developed after four years research at the Hester Adrian Research Centre, University of Manchester. The first set of materials was developed by Hogg et al (1977) who built on the work of Kiernan and Riddick (1973). It was designed for use by staff working with children with severe learning difficulties. During the EDY project an initial pool of 100 instructors (educational psychologists and advisers in special education) were trained in how to run EDY courses so that the package could be disseminated to schools throughout the the country.

In addition to running EDY courses in their LEAs, these instructors also trained co-instructors thus ensuring that the initial pool would continue to grow. To date there are over 500 instructors and at least 5000 staff (trainees) have completed the course.

Surveys of EDY users (Robson, 1988) suggest that trainees and instructors are extremely positive about the course itself and that trainees use the skills learned in their daily work. Formal evaluations have also shown that trainees improve their behavioural teaching techniques following training and can maintain this improvement over time (McBrien and Edmonds, 1982; Farrell, 1985; Bishop, 1989).

Many schools now run EDY courses for all new staff as part of their induction programme. In addition EDY courses have been run with staff who work with adults in a variety of settings such as residential homes, day centres and hospitals (McBrien, 1985). This reflects the fact that the course covers a method of teaching which is applicable throughout the age range.

EDY instructors include educational and clinical psychologists, teachers, nurse trainers and many others. Potential trainees include all staff and parents who live and work with people who have severe learning difficulties.

Successful though the course continues to be, feedback from EDY users has consistently referred to the need to revise and update the materials in order to take account of some recent developments in the field of learning difficulties. Hence the specific aims of the revision are as follows.

1   To recognise the relevance of the EDY approach in adult settings by making the revised version more explicitly applicable to adults as well as to children (including a new version of the video tape showing the methods in use with adults).
2   To bring the package into line with new developments in thinking and practice that have taken place during the 1980s.

3   To show how a behavioural teaching approach such as EDY dovetails into an overall programme plan for a child or adult.
4   To incorporate changes which have been suggested from surveys of EDY users.
5   To combine the old Phases II, III and IV into a completely new Phase II.

However the main focus of the course - to provide practical training in the application of behavioural techniques - remains unaltered. Hence there is a Trainee Workbook, an Instructor's Handbook and two parts to the Demonstration Video Tape (one showing the techniques used with adults, the other with children). Phase I of the course still follows a unit structure with each unit containing a theoretical section which the trainee should read before attending the practical session. The practical session for each unit is the heart of the training, consisting of watching and rating a short piece of videotape, role playing the technique featured in the unit and practising it with a student. Training on each unit lasts up to two hours depending on whether one or two trainees are taking the course.

Trainees who successfully complete Phase I of the course receive a certificate from the Centre for Educational Guidance and Special Needs at the University of Manchester.

We hope that this revision has improved and updated the package so that EDY will continue to be as successful in the 1990s as it has been in the 1980s.

ACKNOWLEDGEMENTS

There are many people who deserve our thanks for giving advice and support in the preparation of the revised edition of the EDY course. Professor Chris Kiernan, director of the Hester Adrian Research Centre (HARC), helped in early discussions on the revision as did James Hogg, formerly deputy director HARC now Professor at the Whitetop Centre, Department of Social Work, University of Dundee. The Manchester teacher fellows, Sue Fagg, Pam Aherne, Ann Thornber and Sue Skelton, also made invaluable suggestions at this stage. Professor Colin Robson, of Huddersfield Polytechnic, provided helpful comments on an early draft of the materials. Jaqueline Doll, educational psychologist in Clwyd, ran a pilot course for staff who teach students with severe learning difficulties in a college of further education and made constructive suggestions for modifications. Dr Eric Emerson's comments on the final section of the Instructor's Handbook were also of value to us.

It would not have been possible to make the child video tape without the support of the staff and students at the Birches School. In particular Marie Morgan, headteacher, and Sue Tinsley, deputy headteacher, helped to coordinate the practical arrangements for making the tape and in running a pilot course. We are also especially grateful to those staff and students who actually feature on the tape.

In preparing the adult version of the video tape and in acting as "guinea pigs" in the piloting of the new Trainee Workbook, we would like to thank colleagues in Plymouth Health Authority and West Devon Social Services. In particular thanks are due to Jacky May (of Woodfield Resource Centre) for helpful comments on the draft Workbook and for participating in the video tape and to Danny Sullivan (of Highbury Day Centre) for co-ordinating practical arrangements over pilot courses and the preparation of the video tape. Similarly thanks are due to Sue Candy (Clinical Psychologist) for being the first co-instructor to use the new Workbook, to all those students and staff who appear on the adult tape and to those who put up with being video taped but could not be included.

Special thanks are due to David Griffiths, senior technician at the Department of Education, University of Manchester, who was responsible for filming the Children and Young People video tape. He also provided invaluable assistance in supervising the editing of both tapes. Without the help, patience and unfailing cheerfulnes of Tracy Timperley, one of the Department's computer staff, it would not have been possible to convert the text into camera ready form for publication.

INTRODUCTION

Welcome to the EDY course!

The main aim of the course is to train those who work with children and adults who have severe learning difficulties to use behavioural methods when teaching new skills. The course is divided into two phases. In Phase I you will receive practical training in how to apply behavioural methods, under the guidance of an instructor. Phase I is divided into eight units, each one dealing with a different aspect of behavioural teaching. In Phase II you will be given training in how to apply these techniques in your own work setting.

The course is not restricted to any one group of staff and hence is suitable for teachers, nursery nurses, classroom assistants, parents, nurses, social workers, psychologists, occupational therapists, speech therapists, physiotherapists, residential workers, day care staff, etcetera.

In this introduction we present a summary of some of the key features of the behavioural approach. We then consider how this method can dovetail into other approaches to living and working with people who have severe learning difficulties. Finally we describe the content of Phase I and II in more detail.

THE BEHAVIOURAL APPROACH TO TEACHING PEOPLE WITH SEVERE LEARNING DIFFICULTIES

The EDY approach, which has its theoretical routes in behavioural psychology, is highly appropriate when teaching children and adults who have severe learning difficulties. By this we mean people who have great difficulty learning many of the basic skills that most people learn with relative ease. Speaking, understanding, eating, dressing and using money are just a few examples. In the United Kingdom children with such difficulties are educated in schools and units for children with severe learning difficulties although an increasing number are now being taught in special or mainstream classes in ordinary schools. As regards adults, it is becoming the norm for those with severe learning difficulties to live in community settings, either remaining with their parents or moving into staffed group homes varying in size from one or two people in a home to much larger groups. Day time activity and employment is varied across the country but typically involves attending a local day centre or sheltered work unit. In some places supported employment is also an option. Despite the welcome trend to community placements, in some parts of the country many adults still live in mental handicap hospitals.

In order to help people with severe learning difficulties to learn, teaching has to be carefully planned and much of it may need to be done on a one to one or small group basis. Generally the greater the learning difficulty, the greater the amount of careful planning required and the greater the amount of one to one or small group teaching needed. As the main focus of EDY is on helping staff to develop their individual teaching skills, the approach is most applicable in settings where this form of teaching is an important part of the whole process of education and development. One to one teaching programmes should be part of an overall teaching plan.

So what are the key features of a behavioural teaching approach as taught on the EDY course?

To answer this question let us consider the teaching methods that are commonly used to teach a skill that most of us acquire at some time in our lives, namely that of **learning to drive a car.** Before the learner driver begins the first lesson, the driving instructor will have a carefully thought out teaching plan which will include the following components.

The instructor will:

a) Be aware of the possible effect on the learner's progress of the traffic conditions, the weather, road works etc.
b) Ask about the learner's previous experience of driving.
c) Know the standard of driving that the learner should reach before being entered for a driving test.
d) Know the components that make up the skill of driving and the order in which they are usually taught.
e) Adapt the teaching sequence if the learner progresses more quickly or more slowly than expected.
f) Demonstrate how to perform certain parts of the skill.
g) Know different ways of helping the learner to master each step in the whole process.
h) Keep the learner informed about progress that is being made.
i) Record the learner's progress so that the next lesson can start at the appropriate point.
j) Encourage the learner to practice driving another vehicle in between lessons.

In this example the driving instructor, possibly without knowing it, is using a teaching method which is in principle identical to many of the behavioural approaches featured on the EDY course. Table 1 illustrates how these behavioural methods are linked to the approach used by the driving instructor.

There are a great many skills which we all learn during our lives which are taught using the same behavioural methods as those that are used when teaching someone to drive a car. Learning to type, cook, wire an electric plug, play a musical instrument are some other examples. Obviously the more complex the task, the more planning is required and the more systematic the teaching should be. **The principles of the behavioural approach** feature in the way we all learn and they are not restricted to groups of people who have specific problems.

As people with severe learning difficulties have particular problems in learning, a systematically applied behavioural teaching programme is required to teach many skills that other people learn easily. For example, most children learn to dress as a result of some relatively straight forward task analysis, prompting, modelling and rewarding. These behavioural approaches do not usually need to be applied in a particularly systematic way for the vast majority of children. However for the person with severe learning difficulties it may be necessary for a teacher or parent to give a great deal of thought to teaching one single aspect of dressing, for example putting on a sock. There are a great many skills that people with severe learning difficulties need to learn which can be taught by systematically applying behavioural approaches.

TABLE 1	
The Behavioural Methods Used in Teaching Someone to Drive a Car	
ASPECTS OF LEARNING TO DRIVE	*BEHAVIOURAL METHOD*
a) Taking account of the weather and traffic	**Observing the Setting Conditions**
b) Finding out what the learner already knows	**Finding the Baseline**
c) Knowing the standard of performance needed in order to pass the driving test	**Defining the Target Behaviour**
d) Identifying the component parts of learning the skill	**Task Analysis**
e) Adapting the teaching sequence as necessary	**Revising the Task Analysis**
f) Showing the learner how to perform certain parts of the skill	**Modelling**
g) Helping the learner to master each step of the sequence	**Prompting**
h) Rewarding the learner for making progress	**Reinforcement**
i) Making a record of progress for the next session	**Recording**
j) Suggesting that the learner practices in another vehicle	**Generalization**

The driving instructor may have been thoroughly trained to do the job well, although this training would not normally include specific work on the application of behavioural techniques when teaching people to drive. However, carers and teachers of people with severe learning difficulties require more **detailed training** in the application of the behavioural techniques, used informally by the driving instructor, in order to increase their chances of teaching successfully. You will read more about these and other behavioural techniques and practice using them with children/adults as you progress through the course.

Hence the core of the EDY course is to train staff to help people with severe learning difficulties to acquire new skills and knowledge. It is a **"how to do it"** course in that it trains staff in **how** to teach using behavioural techniques. These techniques can be applied to almost all areas of life. The course does not set out to advise on **what** to teach

- this decision is left to your own expertise and will depend on the curriculum (in schools) or the content of an Individual Programme Plan (IPP) where adults are concerned. There is plenty of published guidance on selecting teaching goals, for example the Bereweeke goal setting checklist for adults (Felce et al 1986) or the Portage Programme (White and Cameron, 1986) for young children. Furthermore Fagg et al (1990), Ashdown et al (1991) and Sebba and Byers (1992) have considered the impact of the National Curriculum on the education of school aged children with severe learning difficulties.

It should be noted here that a behavioural approach covers much more than the teaching of skills to people with severe learning difficulties. It is widely employed to help people of all abilities to overcome emotional problems, psychiatric illness and behaviour problems and to analyse and understand the behaviour of social groups in terms of, for example, health behaviour, work behaviour and so on. See Remington (1991) for a comprehensive analysis of recent approaches. Your course Instructor can advise on other appropriate literature for those interested in these wider applications. The EDY course must be seen in this context - it is **one** particular application of behavioural methods tailored to the teaching of new skills to people whose primary difficulty is one of learning. The revised EDY course does not cover ways of helping people with challenging behaviour as other highly applicable packages and training courses are available (e.g. McBrien and Felce, in press).

THE CONTEXT OF BEHAVIOURAL METHODS

People with severe learning difficulties have many varied and complex needs just like everyone else. Everybody needs to feel loved and respected, to be a valued member of society and to have opportunities to gain access to all that it offers. Ultimately we all should be able, within the law, to choose what we learn and where we live, whom we live with and what we do. Therefore, when planning services or teaching programmes, teachers, parents, nurses and other care givers should, wherever possible, consult with the people whose needs they are serving and through this provide education and training designed to help them to reach these ultimate goals. This can be done by providing educational opportunities that resemble as closely as possible those which members of society of a similar age would normally be experiencing. Hence specific teaching programmes should form part of a curriculum or IPP which is designed to help a person to live independently in the community. This is in line with the widely quoted "Five Accomplishments" (O'Brien, 1987). These provide a basic philosophy underpinning many services. The EDY course can be seen as focussing on one of these accomplishments, namely that of "competence". This states that many people with severe learning difficulties will require help in experiencing a growing ability to perform useful and meaningful activities with whatever assistance is required.

As far as children with severe learning difficulties are concerned, they need access to the full range of activities that are commonly available to all children. This includes music, theatre trips, school outings, PE, art, craft, design and technology and many more. They also need periods of concentrated work on priority areas from the curriculum and these are usually taught in short one to one sessions or in small groups. Similarly, adults with severe learning difficulties should have opportunities to enjoy the usual range of adult activities in terms of leisure, relationships, work and so on, in addition to being given specific help in learning new skills, again usually in one to one or small group teaching sessions.

EDY techniques as covered in Phase I of the course are most successfully applied in one to one sessions although they can be adapted for use in small group work and in other less structured activities.

These techniques are **one** very important set of skills which will help you to plan and carry out your individual teaching programmes successfully. However, the **first** priority when deciding on a teaching programme is to agree on the person's overall needs and to select those areas from the whole curriculum which are relevant for that person to learn. Only when this has been done should one then choose the appropriate teaching method. Structured EDY techniques will almost certainly be applicable to a great many of these areas. There may be some, however, where behavioural methods form only a small part of the teaching method used.

Finally, although the EDY techniques that you will practice and develop during Phase I are structured and systematic, we hope you will find that the approach looks and feels natural, that people enjoy being taught in this way and that it helps them to learn successfully.

THE CONTENT OF THE EDY COURSE AND THE TRAINING METHOD USED

Phase I

As we have already mentioned, the EDY course is in two phases. Phase I consists of practical training on eight units, each one featuring a particular aspect of a behavioural approach to teaching. There is considerable overlap between units so that during the practical sessions you will get the chance to build on and improve your teaching techniques by rehearsing skills practised in earlier units. On completion of Phase 1, you should have developed and improved your ability to plan and carry out individual teaching sessions with people who have severe learning difficulties.

Phase I carries a Certificate from the Centre for Educational Guidance and Special Needs at the University of Manchester. To gain the Certificate, trainees are assessed by their instructor who forwards the results to the University. The details are given at the end of this section.

Before the start of Phase I your instructor should have arranged a planning meeting to discuss the whole course, the timetable for running the units and any other issues you wanted to raise. **At this stage you should also complete the EDY quiz.** (This is in appendix II along with other evaluation materials).

Phase I is taught either with one trainee to one instructor or two trainees to one or two instructors. Each unit begins with a short written section and study questions which cover the specific behavioural technique pertinent to that particular unit. You should read this and answer the questions before the start of each training session. The study questions are meant to be an aid to remembering the terminology. The answers are provided at the back of this workbook to aid understanding. The training sessions themselves last between one and two hours (depending on whether there are one or two people taking the course) and are broken down as follows (the times apply if there is one person taking the course).

Discussion of the reading assignment and study questions.	5 minutes
Watching a videotape of a teaching session in which the technique is demonstrated and you practice scoring it.	20 minutes
Role play with your instructor to practice using the technique.	15 minutes
Practice with a student, using the technique with guidance from your instructor.	15 minutes
Feedback and plan the next unit.	5 minutes

The first seven units are carried out as above (their format is described in more detail in the Introduction to the Practical Work for all Units). The eighth unit forms the final assessment. You will complete the EDY quiz again and will be responsible for planning and running a teaching session which the instructor assesses.

To complete Phase I of the course sucessfully and qualify for a certificate you should:

   #   Read this Trainee Workbook.
   #   Carry out role play and practice on each unit.
   #   Score 50% or over on the post-course quiz.
   #   Obtain a score of 75% or over on each of the teaching categories on the Trainee Assessment Form (TAF) on the final session (Unit 8).

It is important, however, not to stop at this stage, but to move on to Phase II.

Phase II

This phase of the course is concerned with how the behavioural techniques learned in Phase I can be applied successfully in the setting in which you work. Specifically it covers the following:

   1 The application of EDY techniques to different aspects of people's learning.
   2 Ways in which settings can be managed such that behavioural teaching can be absorbed successfully into all the other activities that may take place.

You will also need to provide at least one example of a teaching programme which you have planned and carried out.

Your instructor will guide you through each of the sections and will supervise you in planning your teaching programme(s).

_____

We hope you will enjoy your EDY course. The vast majority of the 5000 trainees in the U.K. who have already successfully completed Phase 1 are extremely positive about it and stress its relevance to teaching people with severe learning difficulties. Hopefully when you have completed the course you will share their feelings.

GOOD LUCK!

PHASE I

THE EDY TRAINING COURSE

INTRODUCTION TO THE PRACTICAL WORK FOR ALL UNITS: TO BE READ <u>BEFORE</u> THE START OF THE COURSE

TRAINING ON EACH UNIT

As stated in the Introduction, each unit consists of a short written section followed by study questions which should be answered **before** the start of each training session. The practical sessions themselves are run to the following standard format. The times are approximate and reflect the time needed for one trainee.

A   <u>Discussion of the reading assignment and study questions</u>   **5 minutes**

This is an opportunity for you to clarify aspects of the reading assignment about which you are unclear and to go through your answers to the study questions. The study questions are an aid to learning and for this reason the answers are provided at the back of the Trainee Workbook.

B   <u>Demonstration video tape</u>   **20 minutes**

There are two parts to the video tape, one which features children and young people and one which features adults. You will watch the one relevant to the group with whom you normally work. For each Unit 1 - 7 there is a teaching session showing a student working with a member of staff who is demonstrating the particular behavioural technique featured on the unit.

C   <u>Role Play</u>   **15 minutes**

Your instructor will have given you help in deciding which person to work with and which task to teach in the practical session.

Role play will give you the opportunity to take the part of the student in the teaching situation while the instructor demonstrates how to use the technique featured in the unit. You will then get a chance to practice being the teacher with the instructor taking the part of the student. If there are two trainees in the practical session then each of you can take a turn at being the teacher and student.

The aim of the role play is to help you to prepare as realistically as possible for the forthcoming teaching session. Therefore, you should only proceed to the next stage, practice with student, when you are confident that you have thoroughly rehearsed every aspect of the teaching that you are intending to do. The success of the practical sessions depends a great deal on adequate preparation through role play.

D   <u>Practice with Student</u>   **15 minutes**

At this stage you will practice working with the student with guidance from your instructor using the procedure you have rehearsed in Role Play.

Throughout the course we shall refer to the person who is doing the teaching as "the teacher" although we recognise that this could be a wide range of people. We shall refer to the person being taught as "the student".

E   Feedback and plan the next unit   **10 minutes**

At the end of each unit you will discuss how the training session went and plan for the next one.

Note: If two trainees are taking the course together, more time will be needed for role play and practice with student.

EDY RECORDING SHEETS

The two main recording sheets that are used on the course are the **Behaviour Record Sheet (BRS)**, formerly the Qualitative Behaviour Record Sheet, and the **Trainee Assessment Form (TAF).** These are used on all units except Unit 1.

A   Behaviour Record Sheet (BRS)

The BRS is used to record the **student's progress** during a teaching session. You will practice using it on the video, in role play and when working with a student.

B   Trainee Assessment Form (TAF)

The TAF is used to record the **teacher's performance** when teaching. Your instructor will gradually introduce you to the TAF as the course proceeds. You will record the teacher's performance on the video and your instructor will use the TAF to give you feedback on your performance in role play and when working with a student. If there are two trainees taking the course at the same time, you can practice using the TAF on your colleague. Your performance on the TAF on Unit 8 is one of the criteria that is used to determine whether you qualify for a certificate.

Abbreviated BRS and TAF sheets accompany each unit and are for use in the practical sessions. Full size sheets are provided in the appendix and should be used if you find that there is not enough space on the abbreviated forms.

READING ASSIGNMENT

1.1 THE BASICS OF A BEHAVIOURAL APPROACH

The EDY course is concerned with how to apply behavioural psychology when teaching new skills. It is important therefore to understand the basics of this approach. These basics consist of understanding **"behaviour"**, its **"antecedents"** and **"setting conditions"** and its **"consequences"**. In this unit we introduce these terms and concentrate on the role of antecedents and setting conditions. There is more detail on behaviour and consequences in later units.

Behaviour is anything which we do or say which other people can observe. A behaviour is anything from simple events, such as blinking or walking, to complex chains of behaviour such as making coffee, driving a car, writing a letter, speaking on the telephone. When teaching someone with learning difficulties we pay great attention to defining the behaviour we wish to teach. This is covered in detail in the next unit.

Antecedents are the triggers to behaviour. Behaviour does not occur in isolation. We do not sleep, eat, talk, work, drive a car, sneeze, etc., for no reason. There is always something which occurs immediately before the behaviour which is responsible for setting it off. The events which occur before a behaviour are called the **antecedents**. For example, the antecedent to the behaviour of "sleeping" may be "tiredness". The antecedent to "eating" may be "the sight of food". The antecedent to "talking" may be that "someone has asked us a question".

Setting conditions provide the context for the antecedent and the behaviour that follows. For example "tiredness" may occur at night just before bed time. In this case the behaviour of "sleeping" is appropriate. This context "just before bed time" is called the setting condition. The same antecedent of "tiredness" could occur in a different setting condition, for example whilst driving along a motorway. In this setting condition the behaviour of "sleeping" would not be appropriate, although the antecedent of "tiredness" is the same.

Consequences are whatever follow a behaviour. There is always a consequence of some kind. Some consequences have a pleasant effect and these are called reinforcers; some consequences have an unpleasant effect and these are called punishers. It is a basic law of learning that the consequences of behaviour determine the likelihood of our behaving in the same way again. The term "reinforcement" refers to consequences which strengthen behaviour and make it more likely to happen again. For example, if we go to bed early because we are tired and wake up feeling refreshed, then we have received a reinforcer or desirable consequence. In other words, the <u>setting condition</u> might be "at home after hard day's work"; the <u>antecedent</u> "tiredness", the <u>behaviour</u> "going to bed early" and the consequence "feeling refreshed on waking". This (pleasant) consequence means we are likely to repeat the behaviour of going to bed early next time we are at home feeling tired. In our other scenario, it might have worked as follows: <u>setting condition</u> "driving along motorway"; <u>antecedent</u> "tiredness"; behaviour "stop for a coffee"; <u>consequence</u> "feeling refreshed". Once again the consequence is a reinforcer because it was a pleasant or desirable result of the behaviour.

A consequence which is unpleasant and not desirable is known technically as a "punisher". For example, if the telephone rings (antecedent), we answer it (behaviour) and there is an obscene caller on the other end (consequence), this consequence acts as a punisher and makes us less likely to answer the telephone next time it rings. In the EDY course we are not concerned with punishers except to give us a general understanding of their possible effects on behaviour. The best way to teach new behaviour is to use reinforcers (i.e. desirable consequences). The consequences of behaviour, in particular the use of rewards, will be considered in more detail in Unit 3.

The following is a guide to the basics of the behavioural approach.

SETTING CONDITION	The wider context in which behaviour occurs. Examples are: being cold, hot, tired, energetic, cross, happy, ill, in a strange place, with a favourite person. **Example: You are at home on rainy, cold Sunday afternoon.**
ANTECEDENT	The event/s which occur immediately before the behaviour itself. Antecedents are the trigger to behaviour. **Example: The dog whines, your partner pesters you to DO something.**
BEHAVIOUR	What you actually do. **Example: You take the dog for a walk around the park.**
CONSEQUENCES	The event(s) which occur(s) immediately after the behaviour itself. Two main types :
a) <u>Reinforcers</u>	Pleasant results of behaviour. Make the behaviour more likely to occur again when the antecedent and setting conditions are the same. **Example: The dog stops whining and shows affection. You meet a friend in the park and have a nice chat in a cafe. Your partner is pleased.**

b) <u>Punishers</u>   Unpleasant results of behaviour. Make the behaviour less likely to occur again when the antecedent and setting conditions are the same.

Example: You get wet and cold and miss good film on T.V.

The point to remember is that all our behaviour can be analysed according to this model. Learning is a result of repeated combinations of the same setting conditions, antecedents and consequences. By using the behavioural model, we increase the chance that we can not only understand existing behaviour but also teach new behaviours. This applies to us all, whether or not we have learning difficulties.

1.2 ANTECEDENTS, LEARNING AND BEHAVIOUR

Learning new skills relies in part on the learner coming to recognise the meaning of the antecedents. When you first present a small child with a potty (antecedent), it is very unlikely that the potty will be seen as something to sit on and "perform in". The antecedent of seeing the potty has no meaning. When teaching a child to use the potty appropriately we have to pair the appearance of the potty with the behaviour of using it. For example we might place a child on the potty immediately after a meal (a favourable setting condition) and then reward the child for using it. Gradually the child will learn that the sight of the potty (antecedent) is a signal to urinate (behaviour). Eventually behaviour becomes more complex as the child learns to associate using the potty with the feeling of wanting to urinate, as well as with the rewarding consequences of using it. Hence the feeling of wanting to urinate becomes the antecedent for indicating the need to go. In this way children learn to respond appropriately to an ever increasing number of antecedents.

It can sometimes take a long time for people with severe learning difficulties to learn how to respond appropriately to an antecedent. For example, a person with profound and multiple handicaps may have difficulty learning to associate the call of his or her name (antecedent) with the desired behaviour, e.g. a smile or turn of the head in acknowledgement, and with the consequence of the behaviour (reward), e.g. a smile, cuddle, praise.

In the above examples the learner is taught how to respond to new and unfamiliar antecedents. However a great deal of behaviour occurs without ever having been taught and it is not always easy to see what the antecedents are that influence it. For example, parents may wonder why their baby is crying. Frequently they go through a series of possible reasons (antecedents) e.g. the baby's hungry, tired, teething, got a wet nappy, is too hot, too cold, and so on. The parents learn by repeated experience and careful observation which situations (antecedents) lead to crying.

People with severe learning difficulties may not have the ability to tell us about the antecedents which affect their behaviour, particularly "internal" antecedents such as a headache. Finding out what these are is a matter of careful observation. If we fail to do this we may respond to the behaviour inappropriately. For example the person with the headache may sit quietly and not want to join in an activity. We may not have noticed this feeling of discomfort and we may respond by trying to make the person join in, hence probably making the situation worse.

In much of our work with people with severe learning difficulties we need to plan our teaching systematically such that appropriate responses can be learned to an increasingly complex range of events (antecedents). We do this by planning activities that are appropriate to the person's ability and their age and by planning the teaching carefully, using techniques that are covered on this course.

1.3 THE EFFECT OF SETTING CONDITIONS

Setting conditions can be subdivided into:

<u>Place</u>:   home, school, work, etc.
<u>Time</u>:   morning, evening, weekday, week-end, etc.
<u>People</u>:   family, work colleagues, shop assistants, doctors, etc.
<u>Personal</u>:   feeling hungry, not hungry, happy, sad, etc.

Any given setting condition is made up of a combination of the above. For example, suppose it is 5.00 pm on a Friday (time setting condition). You are still at work (place setting condition), attending a meeting with your bosses (people setting condition). You are looking forward to an evening out with friends (personal setting condition). The elements of this setting condition may result in you responding differently to the antecedent of being asked to work an hour's overtime than if this request had been made in different circumstances.

Hence setting conditions affect the way we all behave including, of course, the way we work with people with severe learning difficulties. If you arrive at work having had a row with your partner (an additional personal setting condition to the usual combination of setting conditions associated with work), your response (behaviour) when a member of a group for whom you are responsible asks you a question (antecedent) may be irritable and hostile. This may adversely affect the whole group by making them unpleasant in return. This then becomes a further antecedent which may possibly make you even more bad tempered with your group. It is important to remember that we may not always be aware of how our own problems may become personal setting conditions which affect the way we behave at work and hence the behaviour of the people for whom we are responsible.

People with severe learning difficulties are affected by changes in setting conditions like everybody else. Some may be affected by changes in the daily routine, or by a change of support worker, others may not be. Only careful observation may be able to reveal this. When working with somebody it is always necessary to consider the range of possible setting conditions which might influence the likelihood that learning will take place. For instance a child may be more receptive to teaching in the morning than in the afternoon. Equally, a distractible person may work better in a quiet room than a noisy one. Someone who has recently been given a tranquilliser is likely to be less responsive to teaching. The drug in the blood stream is the setting condition for poorer performance.

An important skill is distinguishing between setting conditions - to know where and when it is appropriate to perform certain behaviours. The technical terms for recognising the differences between setting conditions are <u>generalisation</u> and <u>discrimination</u>. <u>Generalisation</u> means learning to perform the **same** behaviours in different situations (e.g. urinating in the toilet at home <u>and</u> in public toilets). <u>Discrimination</u> means learning which settings are appropriate for certain behaviours (e.g. it is appropriate to hug family members but not strangers at bus stops).

1.4 SUMMARY

1   Behaviour is learned by repeated exposure to certain events in the environment in which it takes place **(setting conditions)**, by what happens immediately before it **(antecedents)**, and by the consequences (reinforcers or punishers).

2   As part of normal development people need to **learn and/or be taught** to respond appropriately to new and unfamiliar antecedents.

3   It is **not always possible to observe** the antecedents or the relevant components of the setting conditions which may be influencing other peoples' behaviour.

4   It is important to understand how setting conditions and antecedents affect **our behaviour** towards people who have severe learning difficulties.

5   People with severe learning difficulties frequently need to be taught to **generalise** their behaviour from one setting condition to another.

6   Conversely they may need to be taught to **discriminate** between the setting conditions in which it is appropriate to behave in a certain way and those in which it is not.

Please answer the questions on this unit before starting the practical session.

STUDY QUESTIONS

1   Our behaviour is influenced by the ...., the .... and by the ....

2   Think of <u>two</u> things which you have done over the last week. Describe the setting conditions, antecedents, behaviour and consequences.

   A i) Setting Conditions...

      ii) Antecedents...

      iii) Behaviour..

      iv) Consequences...

   B i) Setting Conditions...

      ii) Antecedents...

      iii) Behaviour..

iv) Consequences..

3   For <u>one</u> of the above examples, what would have been the effect on your behaviour
     if the setting condition had changed?

     Example A/B: Changed setting condition ....

     Antecedent ....
     Behaviour...
     Consequences ....

4   Setting conditions can be subdivided into the following four components.
     i).........................., ii).........................., iii)..........................., iv)..............................

5   Some people with severe learning difficulties have problems in:
     a) generalising their behaviour from one setting condition to another and/or in:
     b) discriminating between the setting conditions where behaviours are appropriate
        and inappropriate. Give an example of:
     a)... and
     b)...

PRACTICAL WORK

The aim of the practical work on this unit is to observe how changing the antecedents and setting conditions affects the behaviour of the person with whom you have chosen to work.

la VIDEO TAPE DEMONSTRATION (Children and Young People)

The Child:

Kwok Man, aged 9 years, has excellent physical abilities and is generally an even tempered and content child. However, he has no recognisable speech and his comprehension of language is extremely limited. He is also very restless and has difficulties in concentration. If left on his own, he will tend to wander round the classroom fiddling with different objects.

Behaviour and Recording:

Use the record sheet to record Kwok Man's "on task" behaviour. He is "on task" if you think he is using the materials appropriately. Every five seconds you will hear the sound of a bell when you should record with a tick if you think Kwok Man is "on task". If you think he is not on task put a cross. If you have difficulty recording every five seconds, try recording every ten seconds instead. Having completed the chart, transfer your results onto the graph. You should now be able to see what effect changing the antecedents and setting conditions had on Kwok Man's "on task" behaviour.

Antecedents and Setting Conditions:

The video is divided into six sections of one minute each. In each section the antecedents and/or setting conditions have been changed as follows:

A Setting Condition:- Kwok Man sitting at a table with a group of four children.
   Antecedent:-   "Activity centre".

B Setting Condition:- As in A.
   Antecedent:-   Shape posting toy.

C Setting Condition:- As in A.
   Antecedent:-   Musical Box.

D Setting Condition:- Kwok Man at a table on his own near the sink and a cupboard.
   Antecedent:-   Large musical box.

E Setting Condition:- Kwok Man on his own by an open door.
   Antecedent:-   Large musical box.

F   Setting Condition:- As in E.
   Antecedent:-   "Activity centre".

The setting conditions A, B and C were in the morning, while conditions D, E and F occurred two days later in the afternoon.

General Comments:

This video tape only shows a small number of antecedents and setting conditions. What other setting conditions/antecedents could have been used? Discuss these with your instructor and consider what effect they may have had on Kwok Man's "on task" behaviour.

Did you have problems deciding whether Kwok Man was "on task"? Generally this is easier for the posting toy and the "activity centre". However, quietly listening to the musical box is also an appropriate way to interact with the toy and hence should count as "on task".

Ib VIDEO TAPE DEMONSTRATION (Adults)

The Student:

Frances is a young woman with profound learning difficulties. She can pick up and hold objects in either hand but prefers to use her left hand. She can shake and bang objects and can drink from a cup with a little help not to spill. She needs a person with her to use materials appropriately and responds well to praise and affection.

Behaviour and Recording:

The behaviour to be observed in the various setting conditions is "Frances presses the keys of the electric organ such that the notes sound". Count one press each time Frances does this. A new press is counted when Frances lifts her hand off the keyboard before pressing again.

Antecedents and Setting Conditions:

The tape shows one minute of each of four setting conditions with the same antecedent; presenting the electric piano:

A Frances on her own in a quiet room

B Frances with a member of staff in a quiet room

C Frances with a member of staff in a large room with other people

D Frances on her own in a large room with other people

Comments:

There are two setting conditions concerning place (in a quiet room vs in a large, noisy room) - which is best? Frances is easily distracted by other people and sounds. Teaching in a noisy, crowded room is not unusual but this is the situation in which

Frances is most distracted. There are two main types of setting condition: <u>People</u> (with staff vs without staff) and <u>Place</u> (quiet vs noisy room). Which has the greater effect? One minute of each of the setting conditions is not sufficient to make any true assessment of their effect. In reality one would run each condition for perhaps ten minutes and on a number of different occasions. It would also be important to vary the order of the conditions to balance any carry over effects from one condition to the next.

II ROLE PLAY.

1 Your instructor will have given you guidance on which person to work with on this unit.

2 Decide on the behaviour you wish to observe. You can choose any behaviour which is easy to observe and record, for example "sitting", or "on task".

3 Write a clear definition of the behaviour. Some behaviours are easy to define e.g. "on seat" while "on task" is much harder.

4 Decide on your method of recording the frequency of the behaviour. There are several different ways you can do this and your instructor will give you guidance.

5 It is suggested that you choose up to four different setting conditions in which to observe the behaviour and use the same antecedent for each of them. You could try observing the student's behaviour when left alone with a particular task. You could then change this by introducing another person or by changing the seating arrangements in the room that you are using. Again your instructor will help you by suggesting different setting conditions. Use your knowledge of the student to decide.

6 Record the student's behaviour on the data record sheet and transfer your results to the graph.

III PRACTICE WITH STUDENT

Observe and record the student's behaviour using the same procedure as that used in Role Play.

IV SOME ISSUES TO CONSIDER DURING FEEDBACK

1   Which setting condition was the one which most affected the incidence of the behaviour you observed?

2   What are the implications of this for teaching?

3   What other setting conditions or antecedents could have been introduced?

4   Think of some antecedents/setting conditions that occur naturally in the student's home, classroom or day centre. How might these effect behaviour?

UNIT 1 RECORD FORM

Student .. *Kwok Man* .... Behaviour ...... *'On task'* ....

Trainee ... *Beverly* .... Recording method ...... *Every 5 secs. put a ✓ if Kwok Man is on task', a ✗ if he is 'off task'.*

Length of observation ..... *1 minute* ....

Setting conditions / Antecedents		5"	10"	15"	20"	25"	30"	35"	40"	45"	50"	55"	60"	Totals
A	*KM at table with 4 children 'Activity centre'*													
B	*KM at table with 4 children Shape posting toy*													
C	*KM at table with 4 children Musical box*													
D	*KM alone near sink + cupboard Large musical box*													
E	*KM alone by an open door Large musical box*													
F	*KM alone by an open door 'Activity centre'*													

Graph of Results

SETTING CONDITIONS / ANTECEDENTS

UNIT 1 RECORD FORM

Student ....*Frances*.................... Behaviour ....*Frances presses the keys of the electric organ such that the notes sound.*....................

Trainee ....*Julian*.................... Recording method ....*Record with a* ✓ *each time Frances makes a sound.*....................

Length of observation ...*1 minute*..........

Setting conditions / Antecedents		1	2	3	4	5	6	7	8	9	10	11	12	Totals
A	*F. on her own in a quiet room*													
B	*F. with a member of staff in a quiet room*													
C	*F. with a member of staff in a large room with other people*													
D	*F. on her own in a large room with other people*													
E														
F														

Graph of Results

SETTING CONDITIONS / ANTECEDENTS

UNIT 1 RECORD FORM

ROLE PLAY

Student .... Behaviour ....

Trainee .... Recording method ....

Length of observation ....

Setting conditions / Antecedents														Totals
A														
B														
C														
D														
E														
F														

Graph of Results

SETTING CONDITIONS / ANTECEDENTS

UNIT 1 RECORD FORM

Student .... Behaviour ....

Trainee .... Recording method ....

Length of observation ....

Setting conditions / Antecedents													Totals
A													
B													
C													
D													
E													
F													

Graph of Results

```
12 -     -         -         -         -         -         -
11 -     -         -         -         -         -         -
10 -     -         -         -         -         -         -
 9 -     -         -         -         -         -         -
 8 -     -         -         -         -         -         -
 7 -     -         -         -         -         -         -
 6 -     -         -         -         -         -         -
 5 -     -         -         -         -         -         -
 4 -     -         -         -         -         -         -
 3 -     -         -         -         -         -         -
 2 -     -         -         -         -         -         -
 1 -     -         -         -         -         -         -
         A         B         C         D         E         F
```

SETTING CONDITIONS / ANTECEDENTS

UNIT 2

Planning Individual Teaching Sessions

READING ASSIGNMENT

2.1 INTRODUCTION

In the previous unit we looked at how people's behaviour can be influenced by antecedents and setting conditions. For people with severe learning difficulties it is important that we plan and carry out teaching programmes in the optimum setting conditions. By carefully controlling the antecedents we can maximize the chances that learning will occur. In this unit we shall consider some ways in which we can do this when teaching new tasks by using a systematic teaching approach.

2.2 WHAT TO TEACH?

As we said in the introduction, the selection of teaching goals is not covered in this course. However, make sure that targets selected will be useful to the student and will fit in to the overall long term goals as established by the school or care team. Whenever possible involve the student in the selection of targets. You and the student will be putting in a great deal of time and effort working on the selected goals, so avoid trivial, unimportant targets or ones which can never be put into practice later.

2.3 TARGET BEHAVIOUR

Target behaviours should state what the student will be able to do when the task has been mastered. They should be described as precisely as possible. One way of doing this is to follow the structure for writing behavioural objectives. This will be familiar to those who have completed a Bereweeke Course or Portage training (see bibliography). The terms "behavioural objective" and "target behaviour" refer to the same thing. Target behaviours should be written in such a way that they contain the following elements:

* A statement of "who will do what".
* The conditions under which the student is expected to perform the task.
* The criterion of success.

* Who will do what. A behavioural objective must state who will do what. This means being clear about the "what". A helpful way of doing this is to make sure you use an "observable verb". Target behaviours should contain verbs like "says", "writes", "walks", "points to". Having written a target behaviour, ask yourself whether you will be able to observe the student performing the task once it has been mastered. If you will not be able to do this, then the chances are that you have not included an observable verb in your target behaviour. You are probably using a "fuzzy" instead of a clear verb. Fuzzies are words and phrases such as "increase his potential", "become more polite", "understand money".

* **The conditions** under which the student is expected to perform the task.

The target behaviour should state the following:
a) The setting in which the student is expected to learn the task, e.g. in the classroom, the home, the toilet or at the shop.
b) The materials that are required and how they are to be presented.
c) How the instructions are to be given by the teacher, e.g. verbally or with a demonstration.
d) How much help, if any, will be given.

* **The criterion of success.** Having defined a target behaviour, we must also decide how well the person must be able to do it. For instance, few of us would say that someone had learned to select a 20p coin from a pocketful of change if it had only been done correctly on one occasion out of ten. Similarly, we would not say that a person with severe learning difficulties had learned to travel independently on a bus from home to the day centre if this had only been achieved twice out of six attempts. The criterion of success is the number of times the student must carry out the target behaviour successfully before we all agree that it has been mastered. The criterion of success is set at the beginning of a teaching programme.

The criterion of success that you set must reflect the level of mastery required for the task to be performed satisfactorily. The precise level of mastery depends on a) the nature of the task and b) the student's previous performance when working on similar activities.

a) The nature of the task. Tasks where failure to perform satisfactorily might put the student in danger, e.g. using a cooker, require a stricter criterion of success than tasks where failure to perform accurately caries no risk, e.g eating with a spoon.
b) The student's previous performance. Students who take longer to learn things may require a much stricter criterion of success than a person who retains information more easily.

Examples of Target Behaviours:

* John will pull down his trousers and pants in the toilet and urinate in the toilet bowl, without help, when asked "John, can you go to the toilet?", 3/3 times correct each day for a week.
* Tracy will look at the teacher for one second when asked "Tracy, look at me" on 8 out of 10 trials.
* Ataf will point to a 5p coin (from a randomly arranged group of coins containing a 1p, 2p, 5p, 10p, 20p and 50p) when asked to do so by his teacher, 5 out of 5 times.

Table 2.1 provides an alternative way of writing these target behaviours.

TABLE 2.1			
Three target behaviours written as behavioural objectives			
STUDENT'S NAME	*CONDITIONS Instructions /Materials/ Setting*	*STUDENT'S BEHAVIOUR*	*CRITERION OF SUCCESS*
John	"John, can you go to the toilet?"	John pulls down his trousers + pants + urinates in the bowl	3/3 times a day for a week
Tracy	"Tracy, look at me"	Tracy looks at the teacher for 1 second	8 out of 10 trials
Ataf	"Ataf, show me the 5p coin", from 1p,2p,5p, and 10p coins	Ataf points to the 5p	5 out of 5 trials

In the above examples the setting has only been specified for John as it would clearly be inappropriate for him to take his trousers and pants off in any other setting when asked to go to the toilet. In the other two examples it does not matter a great deal where the teaching takes place. Even so it would probably be better to teach Tracy to "look at her teacher" in a quiet area free from too many distractions. Similarly Ataf may initially learn to identify coins more successfully in a quiet setting, although it would be important for him to learn to generalise this activity to a shop.

Clearly then, for some target behaviours, it is important to be specific about the setting in which teaching should take place while for others it may not matter so much.

2.4 BASELINES

Having decided on the target behaviour, it is essential to test how well the student can carry out the skill at the moment (if at all) before you begin teaching. For example, if the target behaviour is for the student to eat with a spoon, you should first watch to see how well the person manages this at present. It may be that he or she can already perform parts of this task, or that it is much too difficult and that eating with fingers would be a better starting point. Finding out how well someone can perform a task is called finding the **baseline**.

The baseline may confirm that the choice of target behaviour exactly suits the needs of the student. However it may suggest that the target behaviour should be adapted or scrapped altogether, because it is too easy or too difficult. The baseline may also give you ideas about the best position for the task materials in relation to the teacher and the student.

There are many ways of establishing baselines. The simplest is to set up the necessary materials, ask the student to begin, watch closely and make notes in your own words. There are more sophisticated methods which involve demonstrating a complex task step by step and recording the student's responses to each one. There will be practice in taking baselines on each practical session in the course.

2.5 TRIALS

In a teaching session the student is required to work on the target behaviour several times. This repetition is very important for learning to occur. The student needs to experience the combination of antecedents (or instructions), their own behaviour of practising the skill and the consequences (or rewards) a number of times before the new skill is mastered. Each occasion that a request is made is called a **trial**. Each trial consists of a request by the teacher, a response by the student and feedback from the teacher. During the trial the teacher may also give help if the student is having difficulty completing the task.

Table 2.2 shows how two typical trials might progress. Each of the headings are those found on the Trainee Assessment Form

2.6 TRIAL PREPARATION AND PRESENTATION

On each trial we try to get the person to do what we ask so that learning can proceed successfully. It is important therefore that the start (**preparation** and **presentation**) of each trial is clear to both teacher and student and that the instructions are given clearly.

Stopping pre-responding. It is important for the teacher to control the start of each trial. To do this the student may need to be taught to sit or stand quietly, and only begin the trial on the appropriate signal from the teacher. You should end all pre-trial activity which interferes with the student attending to the teaching situation. If you do not do this and the student starts before the teacher begins the trial, then it is possible that the student will not understand what is required. This is likely to happen if, for example, the student grabs the materials before the instruction is given. Furthermore it is often necessary for the student to look at the teacher, or at what the teacher is doing, at the beginning of a trial whilst the task is being demonstrated.

There may be occasions, for example when working with a person who has profound and multiple handicaps, that reaching for the materials may be a sign that the student is ready to start work. In these cases it may be preferable to go on with the trial, especially if the reaching behaviour was appropriate for the task. Later on, the student should be taught to wait until you are ready to start teaching, especially when new tasks are being taught.

Demonstrating. This involves a demonstration or model of the task by the teacher. For example when making a cup of instant coffee the teacher may put the correct amount of coffee in a cup thus demonstrating how to do this part of the task. The teacher then asks the student to perform the same task. Hence the demonstration is used to "tell" the student what is required and is particularly important when introducing a new task or a new step of it. For the demonstration to contribute to successful learning, the student has to watch the demonstration carefully and should also be able to imitate. We may have to repeat the demonstration on subsequent trials before learning takes place.

Giving clear instructions to the student. One common reason why people with severe learning difficulties have problems in learning is not because the task itself is too difficult,

---

TABLE 2.2
Progress of a typical teaching trial

Example A: Student (Jane) and teacher are sitting at a table.

PREPARATION: The teacher puts a piece of paper and a pencil in front of Jane and makes sure she is ready to attend.

PRESENTATION: Demonstration. The teacher says "Jane, watch me draw a circle". When Jane is watching, the teacher picks up the pencil and draws a circle.
Instruction. The teacher gives Jane the pencil and says "Jane, draw a circle like mine, here", pointing to a space.

PROMPTS: If necessary, teacher gives Jane help to draw a circle.

RESPONSE: Jane draws a circle, with or without help.

REWARDS: Teacher gives the chosen reward to Jane for completing the task (with or without help).

RECORDING: Teacher makes a note of how well Jane responded and/or how much help she had.

Example B: Student (David) and teacher at the dining table.

PREPARATION: The teacher places two glasses and a jug of water in front of David and makes sure he is ready to attend.

PRESENTATION: Demonstration. The teacher says "watch me fill my glass with water".
When David is watching, the teacher fills the glass with water.
Instruction. The teacher says "David, fill your glass with water".

PROMPTS: If necessary, the teacher helps David to fill the glass to the right level.

RESPONSE: David fills the glass, with or without help.

REWARDS: The teacher gives David the chosen reward.

RECORDING: The teacher makes a note of how well David did or how much help he had.

but because the instructions are too complex. Therefore, having prepared the trial, it is important that the teacher gives clear instructions (verbal and/or gestural) so that the student understands what should be done. Spoken instructions should consist of words or phrases which the student definitely understands.

2.7 PROMPTING AND REWARDING

Once the task has been presented, the teacher allows the student to respond. If there is no response or a partial one, the teacher helps (prompts) the student with verbal, gestural or physical prompts. Prompts are covered on Unit 4. Once the task has been completed, the teacher, rewards the student immediately with the chosen reward. This is covered in Unit 3.

2.8 RECORDING PROGRESS

Once teaching gets under way you should record how well the student does on each trial. There are many different ways in which this can be done. In this course we recommend one type of recording method, the Behaviour Record Sheet (BRS), and you will have practice in using it during each session.

Recording helps you to:

a) Keep a detailed record of progress.
b) Check where the student is having difficulty.
c) Give accurate feedback to the student, parents and other care givers.
d) Share the programme with others who can follow on from where the previous session finished.

Although you may find the BRS recording system awkward to use at first, hopefully, by the end of the course, you will use it automatically. Recording should become a natural part of the whole process of teaching. Examples of completed BRS forms for each of the video demonstrations are given in this workbook. On this unit your instructor will explain the scoring categories to you.

2.9 SUMMARY

1   When planning a teaching programme it is important to set clear **target behaviours**.
2   Before finalising the programme, we should carry out a **baseline** to see how the student approaches the task.
3   A **criterion of success** is set for each target behaviour, i.e. the number of times the task must be done successfully before we can be sure it has been learned.
4   A teaching session consists of a number of **trials.**
5   Before each trial we must make sure that the student is settled and attentive and that the materials are ready (**preparation**).
6   We should start each trial by giving a clear instruction and/or demonstration **(presentation)**.
7   We should **prompt** the student's response as necessary and **reward** immediately.
8   We need to **record** the student's progress by making a note of what occurred on each trial.

Please answer the study questions on this unit before starting the practical session.

STUDY QUESTIONS

1 a) The task we are aiming to teach is called the ....
  b) It must be described as .... as possible and
      contain: i) ...., ii)...
      and iii) ....

2 Write the <u>target behaviour</u> for someone to learn to go by public transport from home
   to the day centre.
   ....
   ....

3 Before starting to teach we should carry out a ....
   to see how well the student can perform the task.

4 In a teaching session the student works on the task for several ....

5 Before the start of each trial the teacher should ....
   and the trial itself should start by the teacher giving a ....

6 It is important to .... the student's progress on each trial.

PRACTICAL WORK

The aim of the practical work on this unit is for you to practice: a) setting clear target behaviours, b) teaching on a trial by trial basis, and c) recording the student's progress on the BRS. Use the session planning sheet to help you prepare (page 41).

la   VIDEO TAPE DEMONSTRATION (Children and Young People)

The Student:

Michael is l9 years old and is in his last year at school. He is becoming socially competent and able to cope quite well in his local community. On leaving school he is due to attend college. As part of Michael's educational programme he is learning to read a number of words and signs that are commonly seen in the community. He had not seen these words before he was filmed.

Target behaviour:

Michael will read the words "Cashier" and "Pay Here" initially to a criterion of 2/2 times for each word (presented consecutively) and then to a criterion of 3/3 times for each word (presented randomly).

Recording:

Use the BRS to record Michael's progress. Your instructor will give you help in how to do this. Having watched the video your instructor will show it again to give you practice at recording the teacher's behaviour using the Trainee Assessment Form (TAF). Use the category PRESENTS.

Comments:

Note how the teacher presents the task clearly and records Michael's progress on each trial. Michael learns these words to the expected criterion of success. Is this criterion of success sufficient? What other criterion could be used? How could this task be generalised? Do we know from the tape that Michael understands what "Pay Here" and "Cashier" actually mean? How might the teacher find out whether or not he does understand these concepts?

lb   VIDEO TAPE DEMONSTRATION (Adults)

The Student:

Lisa is a young woman attending a day centre who is learning, amongst other things, to identify coins and practice using them in shops. She has a daily session of practising with coins and a daily walk to a local shop for generalisation practice.

Target Behaviour:

Lisa will pick up a 10p, 20p or £1 coin from a choice of all three when asked "give me the ....". Criterion of success : 3/3 correct for each coin.

Baseline:

The first part of the tape shows six baseline trials using all three coins. Note that Lisa consistently selects the £1 coin but is uncertain of the 10p and 20p. On trial 3, part of the presentation cannot be heard - the request is for the 20p coin. Does Lisa really know the £1 coin or is she guessing? Jacky sometimes changes the position of the coins but not on every trial - how important is this?

Teaching:

Teaching starts with the target behaviour of selecting 20p or £1 from a choice of these two only.

Recording:

Use the BRS to record Lisa's behaviour on the baseline and during the teaching trials. Watch the tape again and record the teacher's behaviour on the Trainee Assessment Form (TAF). Use the category of PREPARES only. Your instructor will help you to record.

Comments:

Does Lisa reach criterion on either coin? Notice that the teacher, Jacky, always prepares Lisa for the presentation by making sure she is attending and by stopping any pre-responding (reaching for a coin before the instruction is given). Is Jacky consistent in the instructions which she gives at the start of each trial?

II ROLE PLAY

1   Your instructor will have given you guidance in choosing a student and task for this unit. Choose someone whom you know well and who is usually co-operative - the idea is for you to gain practice in the techniques at this stage.
2   Decide on the target behaviour. Make it clear exactly what the student is expected to do. Decide on the materials you will use and the criterion of success.
3   Write out the details on the BRS.
4   Prepare the arrangements for teaching, i.e where you and the student will sit, the position of the task materials, recording sheets, etc. Consider how to eliminate potential distractions, e.g. extraneous noise.
5   Baseline. Demonstrate the task to the student and then ask him or her to complete it. Observe the response, help (prompt) if necessary and reward attempts. You may need to alter the target behaviour if the student is unable to do it at all or completes it without help on the baseline.
6   Try and complete ten to twenty trials.
7   Make the start of each trial very clear by stopping any pre-trial activity.
8   Record the student's progress on the BRS.

9   Your instructor will complete the TAF and use this to give you feedback on your performance as you go along.

III PRACTICE WITH STUDENT

Teach the student using the same procedure as that used in Role Play.

IV SOME ISSUES TO CONSIDER DURING FEEDBACK

1   Was the task too easy or too difficult?
2   Did the student reach the criterion of success?
3   Could the seating arrangements and organization of the task materials/recording sheets have been improved?
4   Did it feel comfortable using trial by trial teaching and recording on the BRS?
5   How might the student generalise from the present teaching situation to work on similar tasks, in other settings and with different people?

UNIT 2   SESSION PLANNING SHEET

NAME OF STUDENT	

TARGET BEHAVIOUR	

CRITERION OF SUCCESS	

REWARDS TO BE USED	

PRESENTATION (i.e. verbal instruction to use, demonstration)	

METHOD OF TEACHING (e.g. backward training, imitation)	

ANY OTHER DETAILS	

BEHAVIOUR RECORD SHEET

UNIT: 2

Score Guide: 4 - Correct / No help, 3 - Good / Verbal prompt,
2 - Better / Gestural prompt, 1 - Some idea / Physical prompt,
x - Incorrect, 0 - No response.

VIDEO DEMONSTRATION: ADULTS

Target Behaviour ....*Lisa will pick up a 10p, 20p and £1 coin from a choice of three.*....
.....*Step 1: L will pick 20p/£1 from choice of both* Criterion ....*3/3 for each coin.*....
Presentation ....*'Lisa, give me the ...'*.................... Reward ....*Praise*....

Step no.	Description	*B* 1	*B* 2	*B* 3	*B* 4	*B* 5	*B* 6	7	8	9	10	11	12	13	14	15
	20p															
	£1															
	10p															

Trials

T= *Jacky*   S= *Lisa*

PRACTICE WITH STUDENT

Target Behaviour .... Criterion ....
Presentation .... Reward ....

Step no.	Description	1	2	3	4	5	6	7	8	9	10	11	12	13	14	15

Trials

T=   S=

VIDEO DEMONSTRATION: CHILDREN AND YOUNG PEOPLE

Target Behaviour ....*Michael will read the words 'cashier' and 'pay here'.*....
.....*presented randomly.*............. Criterion ....*3/3 for each word*....
Presentation ....*"What does this one say?"*.......... Reward ....*Praise*....

Step no.	Description	*B* 1	*B* 2	3	4	5	6	7	8	9	10	11	12	13	14	15
	'cashier'															
	'pay here'															

Trials

S= *Michael*   T= *Anne*

ROLE PLAY

Target Behaviour .... Criterion ....
Presentation .... Reward ....

Step no.	Description	1	2	3	4	5	6	7	8	9	10	11	12	13	14	15

Trials

T=   S=

S = Student   T = Trainee   *B = Baseline*

EDY Course materials, Manchester University Press

TRAINEE ASSESSMENT FORM

UNIT: 2

Score Guide: 4 - Excellent, 3 - Good approximation,
2 - Approximately correct, 1 - Poor approximation,
x - Incorrect, 0 - Incorrect (no action), - - Irrelevent.

VIDEO DEMONSTRATION: CHILDREN AND YOUNG PEOPLE

Target Behaviour ...*Michael will read the words 'cashier' and 'pay here',*
presented randomly. .... Criterion ...*3/3 for each word* ....
Presentation ...*"What does this one say?"* .... Reward ...*Praise* ....

Trainee behaviour			Trials															Data Summary		
	B	*B*																No. of Trials	Score	%
	1	2	3	4	5	6	7	8	9	10	11	12	13	14	15					
Prepares Teaching																				
Presents Task																				
Prompts																				
Rewards																				

S= *Michael*   T= *Anne*

VIDEO DEMONSTRATION: ADULTS

Target Behaviour ...*Lisa will pick up a 10p, 20p and £1 coin from a choice of three.*
.... Criterion ...*3/3 for each coin.*
Presentation ...*"Lisa, give me the ..."* .... Reward ...*Praise*

Trainee behaviour				Trials													Data Summary		
	B	*B*	*B*	*B*	*B*	*B*											No. of Trials	Score	%
	1	2	3	4	5	6	7	8	9	10	11	12	13	14	15					
Prepares Teaching																				
Presents Task																				
Prompts																				
Rewards																				

S= *Lisa*   T= *Jacky*

ROLE PLAY

Target Behaviour .... Criterion ....
Presentation .... Reward ....

Trainee behaviour		Trials															Data Summary		
	1	2	3	4	5	6	7	8	9	10	11	12	13	14	15		No. of Trials	Score	%
Prepares Teaching																			
Presents Task																			
Prompts																			
Rewards																			

=T   =S

PRACTICE WITH STUDENT

Target Behaviour ....
Presentation .... Criterion ....
.... Reward ....

Trainee behaviour		Trials															Data Summary		
	1	2	3	4	5	6	7	8	9	10	11	12	13	14	15		No. of Trials	Score	%
Prepares Teaching																			
Presents Task																			
Prompts																			
Rewards																			

T=   S=

S = Student   T = Trainee   B = Baseline

EDY Course Materials, Manchester University Press

UNIT 3

Using Rewards

3.1 REWARDS AND POSITIVE REINFORCEMENT

In Units 1 and 2 we have discussed setting conditions, antecedents and target behaviours. In this unit we take a closer look at the consequences of behaviour and discuss how these can increase the chances that a behaviour will occur again. This course emphasises the use of pleasant consequences (reinforcers) to help people to learn.

Put very simply a **reinforcer (reward)** is something we like. As most of us like many things, there is an enormous number of rewards which work for us. However as we are all unique as individuals, the rewards to which one person responds are not always the same as those for another person. Most children like sweets and most adults like money. These are two rewards which are common to many people. However some children like sport some do not. Some adults like gardening while others would prefer to do something else. Each person's range of rewards is unique.

When we behave in a certain way and, as a consequence, are given something we like, then our behaviour has been reinforced. If we are reinforced, we are likely to behave in the same way again and hence learning occurs. If we are not reinforced, then we are less likely to behave in the same way and learning will not occur.

Consider the following example. If we make a special effort to cook a nice meal, we will hopefully be pleased with the outcome and those who eat it will thank us and offer to do the washing up! Hence our efforts are rewarded and we are more likely to make a special effort to make a nice meal in the future. However if something went wrong when cooking the meal or if it wasn't appreciated, then our efforts go unrewarded and we are less likely to make the same special effort again. Hence actions which lead to pleasant outcomes are reinforced (strengthened) and those which lead to unpleasant outcomes are not.

Over the years research has shown that people learn more effectively and enjoyably when the emphasis is on reinforcement. Therefore this course emphasises a method of teaching which systematically uses **reinforcement**, in this case the giving of pleasant consequences **(rewards)** for behaviour we want someone to learn **(the target behaviour)**. A number of other things must be done as well if we are to succeed in teaching successfully but these are dealt with in other units.

3.2 EXTRINSIC AND INTRINSIC REWARDS

An extrinsic reward is one which is provided by someone else. Praise, a hug, money, toys, are examples of extrinsic rewards. Intrinsic rewards are not provided by someone else, but come from "within" the person being rewarded. The personal pleasure we may get from playing tennis, or the satisfaction of doing a job well are examples of intrinsic rewards.

Consider a parent who asks a child to tidy his or her bedroom and promises ice cream with dinner as a reward. The ice cream is an extrinsic reward given by the parent. However it is possible that eventually the child will see the benefit of having a tidy room and feel more comfortable in it. This is the intrinsic reward. At first the child may only tidy the room because of the ice cream but gradually this extrinsic reward will not be necessary as the intrinsic reward of having a tidy room becomes more important.

When we start to learn something new, particularly a task about which we are apprehensive, we tend to need extrinsic rewards more, e.g. someone to encourage and praise us. However as we start to master the task, intrinsic rewards should take over. Nevertheless we always need some extrinsic rewards. For example we may really enjoy our work (intrinsic reward) but if the boss never appreciates our efforts or if the salary is low (extrinsic rewards) we may soon cease to be enthusiastic about it.

3.3 FINDING OUT WHAT SERVES AS A REWARD: REWARD ASSESSMENT

As using rewards systematically helps people to learn, it is important when working with someone with severe learning difficulties, to know what rewards to use. Ideally we should use natural social rewards such as praise and for the majority of people this will be sufficient. However some people with severe learning difficulties do not respond to praise and alternative methods may be needed in the short or the long term.

There are three ways in which we can find out what will be rewarding for a particular individual: a) from experience with the person; b) by giving a choice of rewards; c) by offering a series of different rewards.

Experience with the person. Experience of living and working with a person can tell us a great deal. If we know someone well, we will know what kind of things they like and these may be used as rewards. The more closely we work with someone, the better our judgements will become and in this way it is usually possible to decide on the most appropriate rewards to use.

Giving the person a choice (multiple choice). For some people it is helpful to put a few likely rewards in front of them to see which is chosen. Examples of such rewards could be a piece of cake, a small toy or a drink, a notebook, a purse and a clock. If we put three such objects in front of the person several times we can find out which one is preferred by observing which is selected. This may then be tried as a reward when teaching, although there is no guarantee that it will work. Only by working with the person will you find out. Multiple choice reward assessment does, however, help you to decide which one to try first.

Testing rewards one after another (sequential sampling). Not all potential rewards can be put in front of a person at the same time. Social rewards can only be tried one after the other. We cannot give someone a simultaneous choice between a hug on the one hand and our saying "That's good!" on the other as we can do when giving a choice between a favourite object and a sweet. Nor can we give a simultaneous choice between a toy and "That's good!" If we use other kinds of experience for rewards, such as music or showing a picture, we find ourselves with the same problem. Here we must present potential rewards one after the other, that is sequentially, in order to see what effect they have. We may want to try out a cuddle, a teaspoon of yogurt, and showing a bright picture to the person as possible rewards. We would show each in turn a number of times. We would observe signs of pleasure such as smiling, attempts to reach the reward or increased movement. Again our experience of the person will tell us what to look for.

Although these three methods can help us to make an initial selection of a reward, we can only make sure that it will work by finding out if the person responds to it in a teaching situation.

3.4 "AGE-APPROPRIATE" REWARDS

Age-appropriate rewards are rewards which are appropriate to use for any person of a given age regardless of disability. Social rewards, such as praise, are almost always appropriate, so long as we avoid addressing adults as "good boy" or "good girl". It may be appropriate to reward a four year child with a sweet and a cuddle but not a 21 year old. We need to ask ourselves whether it looks or feels "right" to offer a particular reward to an individual who has severe learning difficulties.

Generally the more intrinsically interesting the task and the more able the student, the less need there is to use anything other than social rewards to encourage learning. However there are many tasks which are of no immediate intrinsic interest to the student but which are nevertheless important to learn. This is particularly true of people with severe learning difficulties. In these cases it may be necessary to use a non age-appropriate reward such as a sweet or a cuddle as these may be the **only** ones to which the student responds. Without the use of these rewards the person may not learn. One has to weigh up the balance between the importance of the task with the appropriateness of the reward needed to teach it. If the task is vital, but of no obvious intrinsic interest to the student, then we may have to use non age-appropriate extrinsic rewards.

3.5 GIVING EXTRINSIC REWARDS: THREE RULES

There are three rules that should be followed when giving extrinsic rewards to people with severe learning difficulties. They should be given **immediately**, **enthusiastically** and **consistently**. These rules are now discussed in more detail.

Immediate rewarding. College students will usually work harder if they receive feedback and reinforcement as soon as possible after their assignments have been completed. The same is true for people with severe learning difficulties. Indeed, in teaching trial by trial, it is usually important for the reward to be given within one second of the person doing what is required. It must be clear what the reward is for. If we delay the reward, then we may be rewarding some other behaviour and the person will not associate the reward with the work that has been completed and hence may be less likely to work at it again. If, for example, we are teaching a person with profound and multiple handicaps to pick up a cup unaided, the task may be completed successfully but the cup then dropped on the floor. If we do not reward immediately the cup has been picked up, we will have rewarded the person for dropping the cup on the floor.

Enthusiastic reward. Learning will proceed more rapidly if we use rewards enthusiastically. If for example the student is rewarded by physical contact, then it is likely that a really affectionate cuddle will be more rewarding than a pat on the back. Rewards should be rewarding - not just gestures to show that the student is correct. This is especially true if the task holds no intrinsic interest for the learner or if we are teaching a particularly difficult part of it.

Consistency of reward. At the start of teaching a new task, give the reward every time the student completes a trial. When he or she begins to master it, it may be feasible to reward less frequently, for instance rewarding on every other trial and later still, only at the end of a teaching session.

These three rules of giving extrinsic rewards are especially important when teaching new or difficult parts of a task and/or when a task holds no intrinsic interest for the student. It is also important that the reward gains the student's attention. If the student fails to notice the reward right away then this will have the same effect as delaying it. The student will not associate the reward with the behaviour we are trying to teach. For the same reasons, use the strongest reward that you can find.

As the student becomes interested in the task and starts to master it, the need for strength and consistency of rewards decreases. However it is vital to remember that, even when we feel we can relax the strict rules referred to above, extrinsic rewards continue to play an important part in the way we all learn and should always be used. It is in the nature of having a severe or profound learning difficulty that intrinsic rewards do not work well.

3.6 REWARD PRIMING

At the very start of a teaching session it may be important to indicate to the student that a reward is available. For instance we might give one or two rewards at the beginning of the teaching session perhaps when the student is sitting quietly or for some other simple behaviour which we know the student can already perform. Giving rewards in this way is called **priming**. We are simply announcing to the student that rewards are available. Priming may be particularly useful if the student shows no immediate interest in the task or in the teaching situation as a whole.

In some cases, when teaching gets under way, it may be necessary to prime the student at the start of the trial by showing the reward. This acts as a reminder that the reward is still available. This form of priming should be stopped as soon as possible, since the student needs to attend to the task as well as to the reward.

3.7 EASY AND DIFFICULT REWARDS

Easy rewards. These are rewards that do not take much effort to give. Social rewards such as saying "that's good", smiling and clapping hands are easy because:
a) they can be given immediately,

b) they can be strong rewards when given with enthusiasm,
c) they can easily be given following every correct behaviour,
d) they can easily get the person's attention,
e) they disappear quickly once given.

Difficult rewards. These are rewards that are difficult to give immediately and to co-ordinate with teaching. Certain rewards are difficult to give immediately, for example, letting a child go out to play or taking someone to the cinema. Some rewards are difficult to end, for example a child may not want to stop playing with the toy that has been given as a reward and so it is possible that too much time will be spent with the reward and not enough time working on a task. Other rewards may be difficult to co-ordinate with normal teaching. For example it is not always easy to give someone a drink after each trial of a dressing taskhe.

Nevertheless it is often necessary to use a difficult reward as it may be the only one to which the student responds.

3.8 USING MORE THAN ONE REWARD

There is no reason why more than one reward should not be used. This can increase the attention-getting value of the reward and ensure that the effect is a strong one. If one reward is more immediate than another, then by presenting the easy one first immediately followed by the other, we can reduce the effects of delaying one of them. It is also possible to vary the kind of rewards used in a teaching session. This can help to maintain the student's attention by introducing variety. It can also offset the effect of the student getting too much of a particular reward (satiation effect) - a problem particularly likely when we use food.

3.9 HOW SOMETHING BECOMES A REWARD: PAIRING

So far we have written about rewards in terms of people for whom certain things are already rewarding. If something is not rewarding, for example social praise, we can set about making it a reward.

This can be done by **pairing** something we know is a reward with something we want to make into a reward. Take the example of saying "That's good", a social reward which we may want to make rewarding, and a drink which the student likes. When a trial has been completed we would say "That's good" and follow this immediately with the drink. Note that the reward which already works, the drink, **follows** the new reward "That's good". Many pairings may be necessary before the drink is no longer necessary. For a person with profound and multiple handicaps we may find that we are unable to establish such links and must persist with our known reward. For a more able person, we may be able to start using our previously weak reward (e.g. "well done") and every now and then back it up with our known reward (e.g. a favourite activity). In this way previously known rewards can be faded until the student only receives social praise. Indeed the ultimate aim for all people with severe learning difficulties is to acquire the ability to respond to a mixture of extrinsic social rewards and to intrinsic rewards.

3.10 SUMMARY

1. Reinforcement helps to make learning effective and enjoyable for both student and teacher.
2. **Extrinsic rewards** are given by someone else. These can be social rewards, e.g. praise or clapping hands, a cuddle, food, drink, music, a toy and many more.
3   **Intrinsic rewards** are not given by someone, but relate to the enjoyment the student gets from working at a particular activity.
4. Different people find different things rewarding, and we need to find out what is rewarding for each person with whom we work. This is called **Reward Assessment.**
5. Reward assessment can be done on the basis of our knowledge of the person, from giving a choice of rewards (**multiple choice**) or by presenting rewards one after the other (**sequential sampling**).
6. Extrinsic rewards should be given **immediately** after the student has responded; they should be **given enthusiastically** and **consistently**.
7. Extrinsic rewards can be **easy** or **difficult** to use. Social rewards are easy because they are given immediately and do not last a long time. Rewards may be difficult because we cannot give them immediately (e.g. a visit to a cafe); or because we cannot stop them easily (e.g. a child may chew on a toffee for a long time). Sometimes we have to use difficult rewards as they may be the only ones to which the student responds.
8. We can make something that is not rewarding, or only mildly rewarding, into a stronger reward by **pairing** it with a known, strong reward. To do this we present the known reward after the one which we want to make into a reward.

Please answer the study questions on this unit before starting the practical session.

STUDY QUESTIONS

1   List three extrinsic rewards which operate in your day-to-day life.
   a) ....
   b) ....
   c) ....

2   List three things that you do which you find intrinsically rewarding.
   a) ....
   b) ....
   c) ....

3   Describe three methods of reward assessment.
   a) ....
   b) ....
   c) ....

4   When teaching, rewards should be given :
     a)...
     b)...
     c)...

5   A delay in giving the reward means that you are rewarding something other
     than the ....

6   A reward that can be given immediately and disappears quickly is called
     an   .... reward.

7   A reward which cannot be given immediately and takes time to disappear is
     called a .... reward.

8   Give examples of <u>two</u> easy rewards and <u>two</u> difficult rewards.
     Easy reward ....
                 ....
     Difficult reward ....
                      ....

9   Making something which is not rewarding into a reward can be done
     by .... it with a known strong reward. The known strong reward
     is given **before/after** the weak reward. (Delete 'before' or 'after'.)

PRACTICAL WORK

The aim of the practical work on this unit is for you to observe and record a reward assessment on the video. You will then work with a student to practice reward assessment and pairing of social praise with known rewards. Use the session planning sheet to help you prepare (page 67).

la VIDEO TAPE DEMONSTRATION (Children and Young People)

This video tape is divided into three sections.

SECTION 1 - Multiple Choice Reward Assessment.

The Child:

Tracy is a five year old girl who generally responds well to praise, but needs additional rewards in order to help her to learn.

Rewards Assessed:

The video shows five trials of Tracy being given a choice of a crisp, a drink and a piece of chocolate.

Recording:

Record the rewards that Tracy chooses on the record form provided.

Comments:

Why did the teacher first present the rewards one at a time? Note how on each trial the materials are arranged differently on the tray and how Tracy is only allowed to take one reward at a time. Note that only a small amount of food and drink is available. What has the reward assessment told us about Tracy's preference? How might you use this information when teaching her? What other rewards might have been used?

SECTION 2 - Sequential Sampling Reward Assessment.

The Child:

Nadine is a three year old girl with profound and multiple learning difficulties. It is generally very difficult to assess how she responds to the range of different experiences that she meets each day. She tends not to show the usual signs of pleasure, e.g. a smile or a look which would indicate that she likes a particular reward. Consequently when carrying out the reward assessment it is important to observe very closely how she responds to each of the rewards offered.

Rewards assessed:

The video shows Nadine being offered a bell, social praise/stroking her face, some sweet smelling playdough and a mirror. These are presented three times each one after the other and the teacher makes a note of how she responds to each one.

Recording:

Use the recording sheet provided to note how you think Nadine responds to each of the rewards offered.

Comments:

It is known that Nadine likes food, but because she is on a diet, it is important to try and find alternative rewards which can be used to help her to learn. This section is very short and it is extremely difficult to determine which rewards Nadine favours. To get a more accurate assessment it would be necessary to present a greater range of possible rewards over a longer period of time before one could be sure which reward(s) she really likes. The Affective Communication Assessment (Coupe et al., 1985), suggests a way in which this can be done.

SECTION 3 - Pairing

The Child: Nadine

Target behaviour:

Nadine will look at the bell for one second on four successive trials.

Pairing:

The reward that appeared to be favoured in the sequential sampling session (the bell) is paired with a less favoured reward, in this case, social praise.

Recording:

Record Nadine's progress on the BRS. Then watch the video again and record the teacher's performance using the TAF. Use the REWARDS and PRESENTS categories on the TAF.

Comments:

Nadine's performance tends to fluctuate day by day. On this occasion she appeared to respond to the bell. On another day she may respond to something else. It will probably be necessary for the teacher to continue to pair the known reward (in this case the bell) with praise for a considerable period of time before Nadine will respond to praise alone. In this particular teaching session the known reward (the bell) is built into the task (look at the bell). Other target behaviours, such as reaching, could be taught at a later stage using the bell or another known reward in the same way.

lb VIDEO DEMONSTRATION (Adults)

The tape is in two sections: multiple choice reward assessment and pairing. There is no tape of sequential sampling reward assessment.

SECTION 1 - Multiple Choice Reward Assessment

The Student:

Mark is a young man with profound learning difficulties. He sits only for brief periods of a few seconds and is therefore difficult to teach. He sits much better during meals or when a drink is available.

Rewards Assessed:

The three items selected are a drink of "Seven Up", a piece of chocolate and a tambourine (all known to be things which Mark enjoys). First, Mark is primed with each one in turn to show him what they are. Then they are presented on a tray for him to choose from.

Recording:

Use the record sheet provided to record Mark's choice of reward on each occasion.

Comments:

Which reward did Mark seem to prefer? Note how Peter changed the order of rewards on the tray for each presentation. Why is this important? The tray is rather small. Note how Peter gently prevents Mark reaching before the tray is ready. In reality of course, more trials would be needed to make a true assessment.

SECTION 2 - Pairing

The Student:

Roger is a young man attending a special care day centre. He has no spoken language. In this tape he is learning to identify a cup by name. Roger responds well to praise but this is not usually sufficient for him to attend to a teaching situation. Stronger rewards are needed at present.

Target Behaviour:

Roger will pass the cup from a choice of cup and plate when asked "give me the cup" on two successive trials.

Pairing:

Roger is given social praise immediately he passes Danny the cup. This is immediately followed by a small piece of chocolate (the known reward).

Recording:

Record Roger's progress on the BRS. Then watch the tape again and record the teacher's behaviour on the TAF. Use the REWARDS and PREPARES categories on the TAF.

Comments:

Chocolate is quite difficult to use as a reward - Roger tends to spin it out. Did Danny wait long enough between trials for him to finish the chocolate? Was the pairing in the right order every time (praise followed by chocolate)? How could the use of chocolate be phased out?

II ROLE PLAY

Selection of Student

Choose a student for whom you would like to assess suitable rewards. This should be someone for whom social rewards are not so far effective.

Reward Assessment

1 Select three or four rewards you think the student may like (e.g. music, food, drink, physical contact, favourite object).
2 Decide whether to use multiple choice or sequential sampling.
3 Arrange the seating, recording sheets and rewards.
4 Present the rewards in groups of three on a tray (multiple choice) or one after the other (sequential sampling).
5 Record the choice made each time.

Pairing

1 Use the reward which appeared strongest on the reward assessment.
2 Decide on a form of words for the social praise. Make sure it is age appropriate.
3 Decide on a target behaviour (your instructor can advise).
4 Arrange the seating, materials, recording sheets and rewards.
5 Teach trial by trial and remember to give the new social praise BEFORE giving the known reward.
6 If you think the student is starting to respond to the social reward you may decide to fade out the known reward.

III PRACTICE WITH STUDENT

Use the same procedure as that used in Role Play.

IV <u>SOME ISSUES TO CONSIDER DURING FEEDBACK</u>

1   Did you have any problems in giving the rewards correctly in addition to recording the student's progress?
2   Did the student start to respond to the social reward?
3   What other known rewards could you have used?

UNIT 3 RECORD FORM (REWARD ASSESSMENT)

A MULTIPLE CHOICE

VIDEO: Children and young people

Student ...*Tracy*............ Trainee ....*Maria*...........

Rewards   a = ...*Crisp*............ b = ...*Chocolate*............ c = ...*Drink*.............

	Reward Chosen	Position L, M, R	Comments
1			
2			
3			
4			
5			
6			
7			
8			

(L = left, M = middle, R = right)

Overall preference / comments ....

B SEQUENTIAL SAMPLING

Student ...*Nadine*............ Trainee....*Maria*...........

Note the students response to the different rewards each time they are presented (e.g. ✓, 0, ✗)

Reward Given	1	2	3	4	5	6
Bell						
Praise/stroking face						
Sweet smelling playdough						
Mirror						

Overall preference / comments ....

UNIT 3 RECORD FORM (REWARD ASSESSMENT)

Ⓐ MULTIPLE CHOICE

> VIDEO: Adult

Student ...*Mark*... Trainee ...*Peter*...

Rewards   a = ...*'Seven up'*...   b = ...*Chocolate*...   c = ...*Tambourine*...

	Reward Chosen	Position L, M, R	Comments
1			
2			
3			
4			
5			
6			
7			
8			

(L = left, M = middle, R = right)

Overall preference / comments ....

Ⓑ SEQUENTIAL SAMPLING

Student .... Trainee...

Note the students response to the different rewards each time they are presented (e.g. ✓, 0, ✗)

Reward Given	1	2	3	4	5	6

Overall preference / comments ....

UNIT 3 RECORD FORM (REWARD ASSESSMENT)

Ⓐ MULTIPLE CHOICE

ROLE PLAY

Student .... Trainee ....

Rewards   a = ... b = ... c = ...

	Reward Chosen	Position L, M, R	Comments
1			
2			
3			
4			
5			
6			
7			
8			

(L = left, M = middle, R = right)

Overall preference / comments ....

Ⓑ SEQUENTIAL SAMPLING

Student ....

Note the students response to the different rewards each time they are presented (e.g. ✓, 0, ✗)

Reward Given	1	2	3	4	5	6

Overall preference / comments ....

UNIT 3 RECORD FORM (REWARD ASSESSMENT)

Ⓐ MULTIPLE CHOICE

> **PRACTICE with STUDENT**

Student .... Trainee ....

Rewards   a = ... b = ... c = ...

	Reward Chosen	Position L, M, R	Comments
1			
2			
3			
4			
5			
6			
7			
8			

(L = left, M = middle, R = right)

Overall preference / comments ....

Ⓑ SEQUENTIAL SAMPLING

Student ....

Note the students response to the different rewards each time they are presented (e.g. ✓, 0, ✗)

Reward Given	1	2	3	4	5	6

Overall preference / comments ....

UNIT 3   SESSION PLANNING SHEET

NAME OF STUDENT

TARGET BEHAVIOUR

CRITERION OF SUCCESS

REWARDS TO BE USED

PRESENTATION (i.e. verbal instruction to use, demonstration)

METHOD OF TEACHING (e.g. backward training, imitation)

ANY OTHER DETAILS

BEHAVIOUR RECORD SHEET

UNIT: 3

Score Guide: 4 - Correct / No help, 3 - Good / Verbal prompt,
2 - Better / Gestural prompt, 1 - Some idea / Physical prompt,
x - Incorrect, 0 - No response.

VIDEO DEMONSTRATION: ADULTS

Target Behaviour ...*Roger will pass the cup from a choice of cup and plate.*
.... Criterion ....*2/2*.......
Presentation ...*"Roger, give me the cup"*............ Reward ....*Praise and chocolate*

Step no.	Description	1	2	3	4	5	6	7	8	9	10	11	12	13	14	15
	Roger gives cup to Danny															

S= *Roger*   T= *Danny*

Trials

VIDEO DEMONSTRATION: CHILDREN AND YOUNG PEOPLE

Target Behaviour ...*Nadine will look at the bell for 1 second.*
.... Criterion ....*4/4*....... Reward *Praise and sound of bell*
Presentation ...*Show the bell and call "Nadine"*

Step no.	Description	1	2	3	4	5	6	7	8	9	10	11	12	13	14	15
	Nadine looks at the bell															

S= *Nadine*   T= *Eileen*

Trials

PRACTICE WITH STUDENT

Target Behaviour ....
.... Criterion ....
Presentation .... Reward ....

Step no.	Description	1	2	3	4	5	6	7	8	9	10	11	12	13	14	15

T=

S=

Trials

ROLE PLAY

Target Behaviour ....
.... Criterion ....
Presentation .... Reward ....

Step no.	Description	1	2	3	4	5	6	7	8	9	10	11	12	13	14	15

T=

S=

Trials

S = Student   T = Trainee

EDY Course materials, Manchester University Press

Score Guide: 4 - Excellent, 3 - Good approximation,
2 - Approximately correct, 1 - Poor approximation,
x - Incorrect, 0 - Incorrect (no action), - - Irrelevant.

TRAINEE ASSESSMENT FORM   UNIT: 3

VIDEO DEMONSTRTION: CHILDREN AND YOUNG PEOPLE

Target Behaviour _Nadine will look at the bell for 1 second_ .... Criterion _4/4_ ....
Presentation _Show the bell and call 'Nadine'_ .... Reward _Praise + sound of the bell_

Trainee behaviour	Trials															Data Summary		
	1	2	3	4	5	6	7	8	9	10	11	12	13	14	15	No. of Trials	Score	%
T= _Eileen_ Prepares Teaching																		
Presents Task																		
S= _Nadine_ Prompts																		
Rewards																		

ROLE PLAY

Target Behaviour .... Criterion ....
Presentation .... Reward ....

Trainee behaviour	Trials															Data Summary		
	1	2	3	4	5	6	7	8	9	10	11	12	13	14	15	No. of Trials	Score	%
=T Prepares Teaching																		
Presents Task																		
=S Prompts																		
Rewards																		

VIDEO DEMONSTRATION: ADULTS

Target Behaviour _Roger will pass the cup from a choice of cup and plate._ .... Criterion _2/2_ ....
Presentation _'Roger, give me the cup'_ .... Reward _Praise and chocolate_

Trainee behaviour	Trials															Data Summary		
	1	2	3	4	5	6	7	8	9	10	11	12	13	14	15	No. of Trials	Score	%
T= _Danny_ Prepares Teaching																		
Presents Task																		
S= _Roger_ Prompts																		
Rewards																		

PRACTICE WITH STUDENT

Target Behaviour ....
Presentation ....

Trainee behaviour	Trials															Data Summary		
	1	2	3	4	5	6	7	8	9	10	11	12	13	14	15	No. of Trials	Score	%
=T Prepares Teaching																		
Presents Task																		
=S Prompts																		
Rewards																		

S = Student   T = Trainee

EDY Course Materials, Manchester University Press

UNIT 4

Prompting

4.1 INTRODUCTION

If we have difficulty in learning a task or part of it, we ask someone to help us. **As we become more skilled at the task, this help will be withdrawn until we can succeed on our own.** The help that we receive is called **prompting** and represents an important set of techniques that can be used to help all people to learn. The term prompting is a familiar one in the theatre. When an actor forgets the script, the prompter in the wings provides the missing lines (a verbal prompt). The missing lines provide a prompt or cue for the next part of the script.

In this unit we consider prompting as a means of helping the student to make a response that has not been made before and as a way of reminding the student about parts of the task which they have already learned and have temporarily forgotten.

The types of prompts which can be used reflect the degree of help needed by the student. Physical prompting involves a lot of help. Gestural and verbal prompting involve less help. Elicitation prompts are used to draw the student's attention to the task. **Whatever prompts are used it is important to give feedback by rewarding the student so as to encourage him or her to try again.** The various types of prompting are discussed below. When using prompts, always give a verbal prompt first. If this does not work, give a gestural prompt. If this is unsuccessful, give a physical prompt.

4.2 VERBAL PROMPTING

An example of verbal prompting was given above - the actor forgetting his lines. There is tremendous scope for verbal prompting provided the student understands the words used. Most of us can learn new tasks by being given clear verbal prompts (for example the driving instructor can effectively shout "brake" and most people respond to this verbal prompt appropriately). The most common form of verbal prompt is a verbal instruction or request. In trial by trial teaching, the instruction to begin a task (i.e. the presentation) may be repeated as a verbal prompt to encourage the student to continue with the task.

The complexity of the verbal prompt should reflect the student's ability to understand language - <u>do not use words or sentences which the student cannot comprehend.</u> Prompts should help people to learn and this is less likely to occur if the verbal prompts (or the instructions) are complex and above the student's level of comprehension. It is a common mistake to give verbal prompts which are too long and too difficult for the student. If the student does not respond to a verbal prompt, then it is more effective to use gestural and physical prompting than to carry on repeating verbal prompts which are not responded to.

When using verbal prompts alone it is important to be sure that we are not inadvertently using gestural prompts as well. For example, a student may respond to changes in facial expression, to the direction the teacher's eyes are pointing or to where the teacher's hand happens to be resting. These are all forms of unintentional gestural prompts which we may be unaware of at the time. Unless we can become aware of our non verbal cues or gestures we cannot be sure that the student is responding only to our verbal prompts.

4.3 GESTURAL PROMPTING

Gestural prompting involves actions by the teacher which indicate to the student what is required. A gestural prompt should be given after a verbal prompt has failed. For example, the teacher may indicate what is required by pointing to the relevant materials. More help may be given by moving the hand(s) in a manner demonstrating the action to be performed or the object to be selected. For example, the teacher may make a drinking gesture when asking someone to drink from a cup; or the teacher may point to the plug and then to the socket to indicate that the person is expected to put the plug in the socket.

A more sophisticated form of gestural prompt is eye pointing which can be used to indicate a particular object to be picked up or where it is to be placed.

4.4 PHYSICAL PROMPTING

In many teaching situations the student will attempt to perform but will require assistance. Physical prompting means manually guiding the student through those parts of the task which are difficult to perform. The teacher actually holds the student's hand or wrist and physically guides the limbs through the movements involved. This may range from a simple action such as waving "bye bye" to a more complex task such as writing one's name. Despite the fact that the response has been physically prompted, it is essential to reward the student. In this way the response is encouraged and reinforced.

In physical prompting the teacher must become sensitive to the student's movement and steer it. In order to do this, the teacher needs to be ready to prompt, shadowing the student's hand at a short distance. At no stage should the teacher touch the materials as this will prevent the student from getting the feel of how to use them.

It is important to note that physical prompting is not designed to force people to do something they do not want to do. If the student actively resists prompting, we should review the task in case it is too difficult, or review the rewards we are using. There are some people with severe learning difficulties who do not like being touched under any circumstances and in these cases physical prompting must be used very carefully and alternatives found where possible. Physical prompts should be used after trying a verbal and gestural prompt.

4.5 ELICITATION

If the student shows very little evidence of making an appropriate response, it may be necessary to elicit (gain or draw) their attention. Tapping the task material on the table is a commonly used prompt to draw someone's attention to the task. The tapping is designed to elicit a turning response to the sound with the result that the student looks or searches in the correct place. For example, suppose the target behaviour is for a young child to pick up a rattle. If there is no response following the instruction "pick up the rattle", it may be necessary to elicit this by tapping the rattle to help to focus the student's attention on it.

4.6 FADING

We say that a person has learned something when a new task or part of it can be performed without help. The aim of prompting is to help the student so that he or she will eventually work unaided. Therefore, before we can say that the person has learned, the prompts must be gradually withdrawn. This is described as fading the prompt. The method of fading is from greatest to least assistance, i.e. physical prompts are faded first, then gestural and finally verbal prompts. Different ways of fading prompts are discussed below.

Fading physical prompts. These may be withdrawn by prompting less and less of the action and by reducing the physical pressure applied by the teacher. Aim to fade the prompt from the last part of the task first. For example, a young child learning a ring stack task (see Figure 4.1) would be encouraged (perhaps by indicating) to pick up the ring and then physically guided to the stacking post and helped to locate it on the top of the post (1st stage of fading, Figure 4.1). The teacher would then lighten the grip or actually let go of the child's hand, to allow the child to complete the movement - that is by letting go of the ring. This would be followed immediately by a reward, as if the child had done the task unaided. When the child could reliably do this, fading would be applied to the next part of the task: locating the ring above the top of the post (2nd stage of fading, Figure 4.1).

Fading by prompting less of the task is combined with reducing the intensity. Thus, the teacher may start by holding the person's wrist firmly and then more lightly. At this point the physical prompt is simply functioning as a cue for the student to respond. It can then be replaced by a gestural prompt. In the ring stack task, this could be pointing to the top of the post or outlining the movement of the ring.

Fading gestural prompts. Throughout the fading of physical prompts, the student will have been given gestural and verbal prompts as well. In the ring stack task, the teacher might say "put the ring on", and then indicate by pointing to the ring before physically prompting. When the physical prompt has been faded, it is time to fade the gestural prompt. In this way the student will eventually be responding to the verbal instruction alone. Thus as gestures are faded, the student has to rely more and more on the verbal prompt.

Fading verbal prompts. The kinds of verbal prompts which are used in teaching vary tremendously with the nature of the task and with the student's ability to understand speech. In a complex task, such as dressing, a whole range of verbal prompts may be

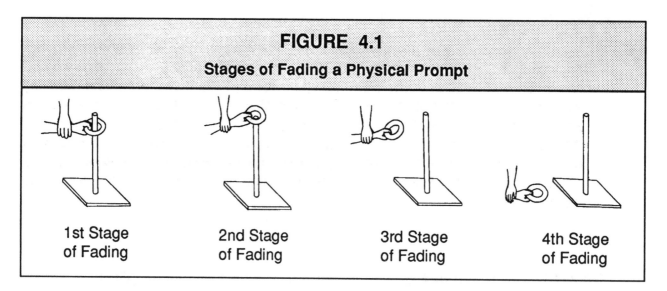

FIGURE 4.1
Stages of Fading a Physical Prompt

| 1st Stage of Fading | 2nd Stage of Fading | 3rd Stage of Fading | 4th Stage of Fading |

used, e.g. "put your arms in", "pull them up", "hold it with both hands". Gradually these prompts will be faded until dressing can be completed with simple instructions such as "put your jumper on next".

Sometimes the student may not understand a simple verbal prompt, e.g. "push". If however "push" is consistently paired with a gestural or physical prompt and the completed response is rewarded, the student may eventually learn the meaning of the word "push" when used in this context. Pairing an unknown word "push" with the physical/gestural prompt and the reward is similar to the pairing of rewards practiced on the previous unit.

4.7 THE TIMING OF PROMPTS

When teaching someone a new task it is helpful to know the person well so that the teacher is familiar with the speed at which he or she usually works. If the student generally works at a slow but steady pace, it is important not to prompt too early but to give the student a chance to respond without help. For people who work more quickly, delaying a prompt may result in the student losing interest in the task or becoming confused by their mistakes. Hence the timing of prompts is crucial. Delaying prompts encourages the student to solve problems unaided. If this is successful, it may increase the chances that what is learned will not be forgotten. However, delaying the prompt should be used very cautiously. People with severe learning difficulties tend not to learn by problem solving but need consistent teaching to master everyday tasks. If left unprompted, the student may not learn the task at all and may become bored or upset by failure. Strong, extrinsic rewards will help the student become motivated and so it is often important to prompt quickly so that the reward can be given.

There is no correct way of deciding when it is time to prompt. Only by knowing the person well and by carefully observing their responses when working on the task will you be able to judge when you need to prompt. In general it is better to over prompt at the beginning of a new task and then to fade the prompts out rather than to delay prompting in the belief the student will somehow get it right without being shown.

4.8 SUMMARY

1   Prompting is one of the major techniques that can be used to help people to learn.
2   The three major types of prompting for teaching new tasks are **physical**, **gestural** and **verbal**.
3   It is important to reward the student even if the response has been prompted.
4   As the person learns the task, prompts should be slowly withdrawn or **faded**. The order of fading is from greatest to least assistance (**physical** to **gestural** to **verbal**).
5   It is important to think carefully about the timing of prompts. Delays in prompting may result in the student making mistakes or becoming disheartened. Prompting too soon may deny the student the chance to work out how to complete the task with no help.

Please answer the study questions on this unit before starting the practical session.

STUDY QUESTIONS

1   Prompting the student by guiding his or her hand is called a .... prompt.

2   Prompting by indicating or pointing is called a .... prompt.

3   Giving instructions is called .... prompting.

4   The gradual withdrawal of prompting as the person learns to do the task unaided is called ....

5   Physical prompts are faded by **reducing/increasing** the physical intensity of the prompt and by prompting **more/less** of the action. (Delete incorrect answer.)

6   The sequence of fading is from greatest to least assistance
      i.e from   .... prompts
              to   ....prompts
              to   ....prompts

7   Verbal prompts are combined with physical or gestural prompts so that the student will eventually learn to respond to .... on their own.

8   We must always .... the student when a trial has been successfully completed even if the response has been prompted otherwise the person will not
      ....

9   Give an example of when you have used physical, gestural and verbal prompts in teaching someone a new skill.
      ....
      ....

PRACTICAL WORK

The aim of the practical work on this unit is for you to practice using physical, gestural and verbal prompts when teaching someone a task. Use the session planning sheet to help you prepare (page 81).

la VIDEO TAPE DEMONSTRATION (Children and Young People)

The child:

Sirshar is a four year old boy who is in a nursery class of eight children with severe learning difficulties and eight children who do not have learning problems. He is generally cheerful, enjoys coming to school and has recently learned to walk.

Target behaviour:

Sirshar will place the following shapes into a posting box when they are handed to him one at a time : a sphere, a cube and an oblong, on two successive trials without prompting. This task is designed to help Sirshar extend his range of perceptual motor skills.

Recording:

Record Sirshar's progress on the BRS. Watch the tape again and record the teacher's performance on the TAF. Use the categories of PRESENTS, PROMPTS, and REWARDS.

Comments:

Note how the teacher fades her physical prompt on trials 4 and 8 and that she demonstrates each new step. Note that handing each shape to Sirshar in turn is an easier task than requiring him to pick from a choice of three on the table. Is the table is too high for Sirshar to see the top of the posting box?

lb VIDEO DEMONSTRATION (Adults)

The tape is in two sections.

SECTION 1

The Student:

Roger is the young man seen on Unit 3 working on the same task (identifying a cup). To help Roger to generalise this skill, staff make a point of stressing the word "cup" during mealtimes and drinks.

Target Behaviour:

Roger will give the cup from a choice of a cup and plate when asked "give me the cup". Criterion of success 2/2. Note that the PRESENTATION of this task includes a gesture of Danny holding out his hands as well as the verbal instruction "give me the cup".

Recording:

Record Roger's progress on the BRS. Watch the tape again and record on the TAF. This time use the TAF categories of PREPARES, PROMPTS and REWARDS. If this is too difficult, use PROMPTS and one other category.

Comments:

Note how Danny gains Roger's attention at the start of each trial (part of the PREPARES category). Danny uses two types of gesture to help Roger to respond - he holds out his hands as part of the PRESENTATION of the task and later in the trial he points to the cup (a gestural prompt). Verbal prompting is kept very simple in line with Roger's level of ability. Physical prompts are not required to help Roger to grasp or pick up the cup, but very slight physical prompts are used to guide his hand towards it.

SECTION 2

Mark (from Unit 3) appears again on this short section of tape which is designed to illustrate a full physical prompt using hand over hand guidance. The task is to teach Mark to feed himself with a spoon. There is no need to record this section. Observe how the teacher (Steve) uses full prompting on three parts of the task: he prompts Mark to grip the spoon correctly, he prompts him to scoop food onto the spoon, and finally he prompts Mark to return the spoon to the table. Mark takes the spoon up to his mouth, takes the food from the spoon and the spoon from his mouth without help. The same sequence is seen when Mark takes a drink. Note how Steve shadows Mark's hand so as to be ready to prompt immediately if necessary.

II ROLE PLAY

    1   Selection of student: choose a student who is ready to learn a task which will require physical, gestural and verbal prompting in order to encourage learning.

    2   Write the target behaviour.

    3   Decide on the appropriate reward/s (do a reward assessment if necessary).

    4   Prepare the seating arrangements, task materials, rewards and recording sheets.

    5   Carry out one or two baseline trials at the start of the teaching session.

    6   Decide exactly how you intend to use physical, gestural and verbal prompts.

    7   Teach on a trial by trial basis and record the learner's progress on the BRS.

    8   Consider how prompts will be faded.

    9   Think carefully about the timing of prompts on each trial.

    10   Your instructor will guide you through the practical session and will record your performance on the TAF.

III PRACTICE WITH STUDENT

Teach the student using the same procedure as that used in Role Play.

IV <u>SOME ISSUES TO CONSIDER DURING FEEDBACK</u>

1   Were you always aware when you were prompting? Sometimes we may **think** that a person has performed a task unaided but we were unaware that we had used a slight gestural or verbal prompt.

2   Did you **time** your prompts in such a way as to give the student the chance to do the task unaided?

3   Or did you delay your prompts so the student made too many mistakes or lost interest in the task?

4   Did you manage to avoid physically prompting the materials?

5   Some tasks are very difficult to teach using physical prompts, e.g. doing up buttons, vocalizing. Can you think of others that fall into this category?

UNIT 4   SESSION PLANNING SHEET

NAME OF STUDENT

TARGET BEHAVIOUR

CRITERION OF SUCCESS

REWARDS TO BE USED

PRESENTATION (i.e. verbal instruction to use, demonstration)

METHOD OF TEACHING (e.g. backward training, imitation)

ANY OTHER DETAILS

Score Guide: 4 - Correct / No help, 3 - Good / Verbal prompt,
2 - Better / Gestural prompt, 1 - Some idea / Physical prompt,
x - Incorrect, 0 - No response.

BEHAVIOUR RECORD SHEET

UNIT: 4

VIDEO DEMONSTRATION: CHILDREN AND YOUNG PEOPLE

Target Behaviour *Sirshar will place a sphere, a cube and an oblong*
into a posting box. Criterion 2/2 Reward *Praise*
Presentation *Put this one in*

Step no.	Description	B											Trials			
		1	2	3	4	5	6	7	8	9	10	11	12	13	14	15
1	*Post* ○ □															
2	*Post* ○ □ □															

S= *Doreen*   T= *Sirshar*

VIDEO DEMONSTRATION: ADULTS

Target Behaviour *Roger will pass the cup from a choice of cup and plate.*
Criterion 2/2 Reward *Praise and chocolate*
Presentation *"Roger, give me the cup"*

Step no.	Description												Trials			
		1	2	3	4	5	6	7	8	9	10	11	12	13	14	15
1	*Roger gives cup to Danny*															

S= *Roger*   T= *Danny*

ROLE PLAY

Target Behaviour ....
Criterion .... Reward ....
Presentation ....

Step no.	Description												Trials			
		1	2	3	4	5	6	7	8	9	10	11	12	13	14	15

S=   T=

PRACTICE WITH STUDENT

Target Behaviour ....
Criterion .... Reward ....
Presentation ....

Step no.	Description												Trials			
		1	2	3	4	5	6	7	8	9	10	11	12	13	14	15

S=   T=

S = Student   T = Trainee   B = Baseline

EDY Course materials, Manchester University Press

Score Guide: 4 - Excellent, 3 - Good approximation,
2 - Approximately correct, 1 - Poor approximation,
x - Incorrect, 0 - Incorrect (no action), - - Irrelevent.

TRAINEE ASSESSMENT FORM   UNIT: 4

VIDEO DEMONSTRATION: CHILDREN AND YOUNG PEOPLE

Target Behaviour ...Sirshar will place a sphere, a cube and an oblong into a posting box.
Criterion 2/2
Presentation ..."Put this one in"   Reward ...Praise

Trainee behaviour	B	Trials 1	2	3	4	5	6	7	8	9	10	11	12	13	14	15	Data Summary No. of Trials	Score	%
Prepares Teaching																			
Presents Task																			
Prompts																			
Rewards																			

T= Doreen   S= Sirshar

VIDEO DEMONSTRTION: ADULTS

Target Behaviour ...Roger will pass the cup from a choice of cup and plate.
Criterion 2/2
Presentation ..."Roger, give me the cup"   Reward ...Praise and chocolate

Trainee behaviour	Trials 1	2	3	4	5	6	7	8	9	10	11	12	13	14	15	Data Summary No. of Trials	Score	%
Prepares Teaching																		
Presents Task																		
Prompts																		
Rewards																		

T= Danny   S= Roger

ROLE PLAY

Target Behaviour ....   Criterion ....
Presentation ....   Reward ....

Trainee behaviour	Trials 1	2	3	4	5	6	7	8	9	10	11	12	13	14	15	Data Summary No. of Trials	Score	%
Prepares Teaching																		
Presents Task																		
Prompts																		
Rewards																		

T=   S=

PRACTICE WITH STUDENT

Target Behaviour ....   Criterion ....
Presentation ....   Reward ....

Trainee behaviour	Trials 1	2	3	4	5	6	7	8	9	10	11	12	13	14	15	Data Summary No. of Trials	Score	%
Prepares Teaching																		
Presents Task																		
Prompts																		
Rewards																		

T=   S=

S = Student   T = Trainee   B = Baseline

EDY Course Materials, Manchester University Press

Task Analysis

5.1 INTRODUCTION

In previous units we stressed the importance of setting clear target behaviours when planning teaching programmes. Even an apparently simple target behaviour may be very complicated for someone to learn unless we break it down into smaller steps. Breaking a task down into smaller steps is called **Task Analysis.** Careful task analysis helps the student to master the task step by step. In this way learning is more likely to occur because small steps can be achieved and rewarded. In addition, the teacher can see clearly how much progress is being made.

5.2 BREAKING THE TASK INTO STEPS

There are four stages we must go through when analysing a task. First, describe the target behaviour exactly. Second, describe the steps leading to the target behaviour. Third, carry out several baselines on the steps with the student. Fourth, revise the task analysis according to the individual student's baseline response. It may be necessary to repeat the baseline on the revised steps. The steps should include all parts of the task which are necessary for the student to reach the target behaviour.

5.3 EXAMPLE OF A TASK ANALYSIS : USING AN ELECTRIC KETTLE

Target behaviour : when presented with an empty electric kettle (Figure 5.1) and asked to fill it up to the "maximum" mark, plug it in and switch it on, the student performs the task correctly once a day for a week.

Figure 5.1 shows the kettle, the lead lying next to it, the electric socket and the sink. For this task analysis the exact position of these objects is not important provided the student knows where the sink and the socket are.

Figure 5.2 illustrates one way to analyse this task into small steps - five in this case. There are other ways to analyse the same task. The exact nature and number of the steps will depend on the ability of the person you are teaching. (Note: This kettle is designed so that it can be filled without having to take off the lid.)

Although each step could be taught on its own, in order for the student to learn how the whole task is linked together, it is important for each new step to incorporate the previous

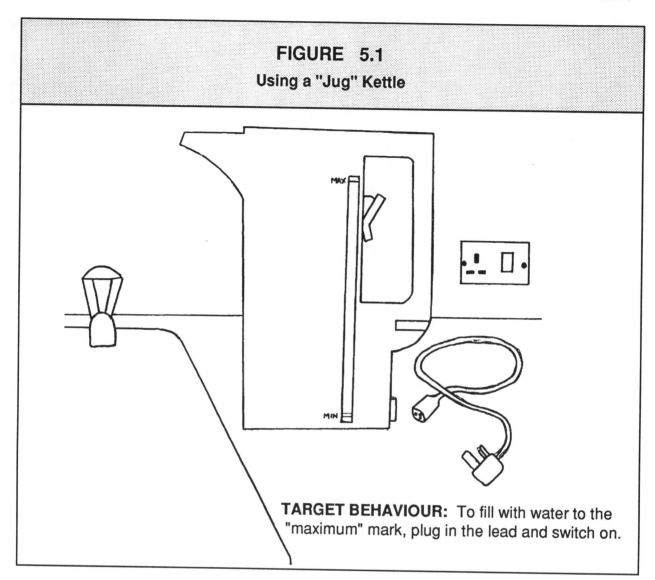

FIGURE 5.1
Using a "Jug" Kettle

TARGET BEHAVIOUR: To fill with water to the "maximum" mark, plug in the lead and switch on.

ones. Hence when working on Step 2, placing the lead into the kettle, the student would also carry out Step 1 first, filling the kettle with water.

When planning your task analysis it is important to ask yourself whether it is essential to keep to the order of steps or not. Some steps may <u>have</u> to be done before others (e.g. for safety reasons), for other steps there may be a choice. During the baseline, the student may show an inclination to learn the steps in a particular order different from the one planned. This may be fine, in which case re-order the task analysis. Once the order of steps has been finalised, this order should be kept to and and everyone should teach the steps in the agreed order.

5.4 BASELINES AND TASK ANALYSIS

Baseline. Any task we want to teach can be broken down into small steps. It is quite possible to have as many as 12 steps in a task analysis or only four or five. A step can be very small (e.g. lift arm from table) or quite complex (e.g. tie a knot). The number and size of steps depends on how well the person can do the task before you start teaching. The best method of finding this out is to make a rough task analysis (using the Task Analysis Baseline Recording Sheet) and carry out a **baseline on these steps.**

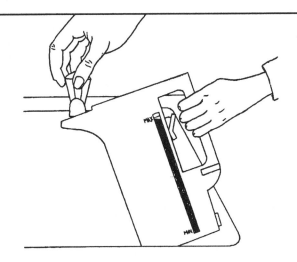

STEP 1: Fill the kettle with water to the maximum mark

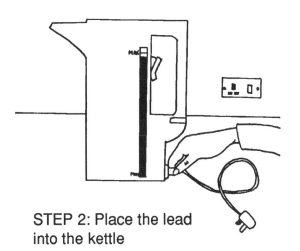

STEP 2: Place the lead into the kettle

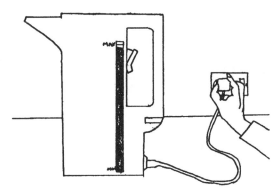

STEP 3: Place the plug in the wall

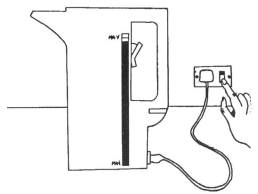

STEP 4: Switch on at the wall

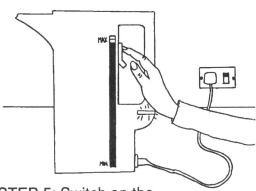

STEP 5: Switch on the kettle

FIGURE 5.2

Task Analysis for Using a

"Jug" Kettle

Set out the task materials and ask the student to try the task by giving a clear instruction. Note down against each step how well the student does (you can use the BRS scoring). If the student is stuck, give prompts and demonstrations as necessary and note down the response. Use this baseline information to make a full task analysis suited to the individual needs of the student. You may then need to repeat the baseline on the revised steps a number of times before finalising the teaching plan.

It is important to reward the student after each baseline so as to keep his or her interest in the task.

Teaching step by step. When you are satisfied that the nature, number and order of steps in your task analysis are appropriate, then you are ready to begin teaching on a step by step basis. As with setting clear target behaviours, it is important to **set a criterion of success** for each step of the task so that you know when to move on to the next step. Let us suppose that for the kettle task the criterion has been set at two out of two (2/2) correct responses for each step.

When teaching the steps, use the BRS recording system. For example, on Step 1 (filling the kettle), if the step was demonstrated and the student succeeded with no more help, write a "3" on the BRS. If a physical prompt was needed, record with a "1". When the student has done this step correctly with no help on two consecutive occasions (i.e. two "4s" in a row have been scored) the agreed criterion of success has been reached. You can then move on to the next step. In this way, you can move through all the steps. This may take several teaching sessions.

5.5 WHAT TO DO IF THE STUDENT DOES NOT SUCCEED

Your BRS may show that the student is having difficulty in learning a particular step. If a score of 1 is obtained on four or five consecutive trials (i.e. the student has been getting a physical prompt on each of these trials), then there is something wrong. There may be several reasons why learning is not taking place:

a)   The teacher may be confusing the student by not presenting the task clearly. The materials may be in a muddle or the teacher may be distracting the student by using inappropriate language or by fumbling.
b)   The promptong may be inaccurate or poorly done.
c)   The student may be finding the whole teaching session unrewarding resulting in him or her losing interest or appearing fed up.
d)   The step may be too difficult. Even if the above are being done correctly, the step may be so difficult that the student cannot master it.

Suggested solutions

a)   **Present the trial again** making sure, i) the student is attending before you start; ii) you have the materials set out correctly and there are no distractions; iii) you give a very clear instruction - this might be a verbal signal or might include a demonstration of the step; iv) your prompting is clear and helpful.
b)   If the above does not work, **go back to the previous step** which has already been learned. If the student fails on this step as well, then perhaps the reward is no longer effective.

c) If the student no longer feels rewarded for working on the task, **try using a different reward** or increase the strength of the rewards you are already using. If necessary remove the task materials and carry out a reward assessment (see Unit 3).

d) If none of the above is effective, the problem may lie in the present step being too difficult. Try doing some **more task analysis** on this step; break it down into two or more simpler steps. For example, if the student was stuck on Step 1 of the kettle task (filling the kettle to the "maximum" mark, see Figure 5.2) and you had checked that the task presentation and rewards were correct, you could analyse this step further. Filling the kettle with water to the correct point (i.e. Step 1) is quite a complex task in itself and requires the person to hold the kettle under the correct tap with one hand while turning on the tap with the other. The kettle has to be held steady and the tap turned off when the water level has reached the correct point. This part of the kettle task could be broken down into several steps. Having decided on how you would break the step down, possibly by doing more baseline trials on this step, teach it and record in the way already mentioned until the student has mastered it and is ready to rejoin the original task analysis.

5.6 SUMMARY

1   Many things that we want to teach are too complicated to learn in one step and need to be broken down into smaller steps.
2   To break tasks down we have to decide exactly what we want to teach (**target behaviour**) and what skills the person has to master to succeed in that target behaviour (the steps).
3   Breaking a task down into steps or sub-skills is called **Task Analysis**. Effective task analysis results in steps being small enough for the student to make progress.
4   We can break down any task in this way however simple or complex it appears.
5   When planning a task analysis we should carry out a **baseline** to assess the person's present level of ability on the task and make notes on what parts can and cannot be done.
6   In teaching the task it is important to set a **criterion of success** for each step.
7   If the student does not show progress on a particular step, we must check that the presentation and prompting of the task are clear, that the student still finds the teaching situation rewarding, that the previous step has not been forgotten and that the present step is not too difficult. If the step is too difficult, further task analysis can be done to make it simpler.

Please answer the study questions on this unit before starting the practical session.

STUDY QUESTIONS

1   Breaking a task down into its component parts is called
    ....

2   We break a task down into manageable steps because otherwise it will be
    too .... for the person to learn.

3   There are four stages we must go through when breaking down a task. They are
    a) Describe the .... exactly.
    b) Describe the essential .... which go to make up (a).
    c) Carry out a number of ....
    d) Revise the ....

4   When teaching a task do not move on to the next step until the student has
    ....

5   What should you do if the student is not making progress on a particular step.
    a)...
    b)...
    c)...
    d)...

PRACTICAL WORK

PREPARATION BEFORE SESSION

The aim of the practical work on this unit is for you to practice making a task analysis, carry out baselines, revise the steps and begin teaching on the selected steps. Use the Session Planning Sheet to help you prepare for the practical.

This practical session can take longer than for other units because a) the video tape work is longer and b) preparing a task analysis and baselines can take a long time, particularly if initial ideas for a target behaviour prove unsuitable. Therefore, if at all possible, BEFORE coming to the practical session :

1   Choose a student to work with who is ready to learn a task once it has been broken down into steps.
2   Decide on the target behaviour.
3   Think of different ways in which your task could be analysed.
4   Write down the task analysis on the **Task Analysis Baseline Recording Sheet** (page 105)
5   Conduct one or two baseline trials with the student before the start of the practical session and revise the task analysis accordingly. (Use the Task Analysis Baseline Recording Sheet to help you to do this. Further copies are available at the end of this workbook).

la <u>VIDEO TAPE DEMONSTRATION (Children and Young People).</u>

The Student:

Sarika is l6 years old and has cerebral palsy which affects her ability to walk and to use her left hand. Normally she is a cheerful and talkative person although she is extremely quiet on the video tape, possibly because of the unfamiliar setting condition created by being filmed.

Target Behaviour:

Sarika will load a cassette tape into the "Walkman" and listen to it through the headphones on two successive trials with the teacher steadying the tape recorder. This is the first time Sarika had been introduced to the "Walkman". As she enjoys music it is hoped that learning this task will increase her range of options for leisure activities.

Task Analysis:

In the first section of the video, the teacher demonstrates the steps of the task as below:

> Step 1 Lift the "lid" of the "Walkman".
> Step 2 Put the tape in.
> Step 3 Close the "lid".
> Step 4 Plug the lead into the "Walkman".
> Step 5 Put the headphones on.
> Step 6 Press the "Play" button.

Recording:

The remainder of the tape is in three sections. In the first section, the baseline, the teacher demonstrates all but the last step and then asks Sarika to do the whole task. Use the **Task Analysis Baseline Recording Sheet** to record Sarika's performance on the baseline trial.

In the second section Sarika is learning the first two steps of the task. Use the BRS to record her progress.

In the final section the task has been broken down further in that Step 2, "put the tape in", has been divided into two further steps. Again record Sarika's progress on a separate part of the BRS.

Having watched the video your instructor will play the second or third section again to give you a chance to practice using the TAF. Try to use ALL categories on TAF but if this is difficult concentrate on PREPARES and one other.

Comments:

Despite Sarika's quietness during this session, she clearly enjoyed learning how to play the Walkman. Her cerebral palsy is obviously a factor which may impede further progress in learning this task. In order to take account of this, the teacher positioned and held the Walkman to help Sarika complete different parts of the task. This help would have to be withdrawn before Sarika could complete the task independently.

Note how the teacher clearly demonstrated and presented the task to Sarika. Are there any other ways in which this task could be analysed which would take account of Sarika's physical difficulties? Should the steps have been taught in a different order?

lb VIDEO DEMONSTRATION (Adults)

The video tape is in two sections.

SECTION 1 - Baseline on placing batteries in cassette.

The Student:

Alan is keen on music and is able to operate the tape recorder. Staff were interested to know if he could also change the batteries.

Target Behaviour:

Alan will put new batteries into his tape recorder.

Baseline and Recording:

The tape shows a baseline of the target behaviour. To staff's suprise Alan shows himself very competent. Watch the tape and write down the steps which Alan went through to achieve the target behaviour. Use the **Task Analysis Baseline Recording Sheet** in the

Workbook. Watch the tape again and score Alan on each step.

Comments:

How many steps in your task analysis? Which steps does Alan need some teaching on? What criterion of success would you set for each step?

SECTION 2 - Task Analysis and Teaching of Tying Shoe Laces

The Student:

Alan appears again here, this time on a task which he is ready and keen to learn.

Target Behaviour:

Alan will tie his shoe laces with shoe on the table. Criterion of success for each step 3/3.

Scoring the Baseline:

The steps which his teacher Jacky has decided upon are written in the Workbook and Jacky speaks them aloud on the tape. Watch the tape and then score Alan on each step during the baseline. Notice that on the BRS the revised steps are shown - these are the steps which are going to be taught.

Recording the teaching:

Score Alan's progress on each step which is taught. Trial 5 may be confusing - it is a very long trial. Watch the tape again and score Jacky's teaching on the TAF. Use ALL the categories this time. If this is too difficult, score PRESENTS and PROMPTS.

Comments:

Does Alan reach criterion on Step 1 before going on to Step 2? Notice how on trials 5 and 6 Alan scores only 1. On trial 7 Jacky changes her presentation by making a larger loop and by suggesting the loop is held to one side. This seems to be effective in enabling Alan to make progress. What else could she have done? We do not see on the video Alan reaching criterion on step 2 - this is in the interests of keeping the tape relatively short and yet showing a little of step 3.

II ROLE PLAY

1 Revise the task analysis in light of the baseline and discussion with your instructor.
2 Decide on the criterion of success for each step. This may be the same as the criterion of success for the whole task, although not necessarily.
3 Teach the student on a trial by trial basis as practiced in the previous units.
4 Record the student's progress on each trial on the BRS.

5 Your instructor will help you through the practical session by giving feedback based
   on the TAF.

III PRACTICE WITH STUDENT

Teach the student using the same procedure as that used in Role Play.

IV SOME ISSUES TO CONSIDER DURING FEEDBACK

1   Was the task too easy or too difficult?
2   Was the task analysis appropriate?
3   Were the steps taught in the correct order?
4   How will you teach the student to work on this and similar tasks
     in other settings and with different people?

UNIT 5   SESSION PLANNING SHEET

NAME OF STUDENT

TARGET BEHAVIOUR

CRITERION OF SUCCESS

REWARDS TO BE USED

PRESENTATION (i.e. verbal instruction to use, demonstration)

METHOD OF TEACHING (e.g. backward training, imitation)

ANY OTHER DETAILS

TASK ANALYSIS BASELINE RECORDING SHEET

Student .... *Sarika* .... Trainee .... *Barbara* ....
Target Behaviour.. *Sarika will load a tape into the 'Walkman' (with the teacher steadying it) and listen to it*
.. *through the headphones.* ....
Presentation.. *'Sarika, can you play the tape' (or similar)* .... Criterion.... *2/2* ....
Reward.. *Praise and music* ....

Steps No.		Description	Baseline Trials				
Init.	Rev.		1	2	3	4	5
1		Lift the 'lid' of the 'Walkman'					
2		Put the tape in					
3		Close the 'lid'					
4		Plug the lead into the 'Walkman'					
5		Put the headphones on					
6		Press the 'play' button					
7							
8							
9							
10							

Score Guide: 4 - Correct / No help
3 - Good / Verbal prompt
2 - Better / Gestural prompt
1 - Some idea / Physical prompt
x - Incorrect. 0 - No response

Init. = Initial steps suggested from the task analysis
Rev. = Revised steps following baseline observations.

EDY Course materials, Manchester University Press.

TASK ANALYSIS BASELINE RECORDING SHEET

Student ...*Alan*.................................... Trainee *Steve*.....................................
Target Behaviour...*Alan will put new batteries into his tape recorder.*.....................
.... Criterion.... ....
Presentation.*'Alan, can you put the batteries in' (or similar)* Reward..*Praise*.................

Steps No.		Description	Baseline Trials				
Init.	Rev.		1	2	3	4	5
1							
2							
3							
4							
5							
6							
7							
8							
9							
10							

Score Guide: 4 - Correct / No help
3 - Good / Verbal prompt
2 - Better / Gestural prompt
1 - Some idea / Physical prompt
x - Incorrect. 0 - No response

<u>Init.</u> = Initial steps suggested from the task analysis
<u>Rev.</u> = Revised steps following baseline observations.

EDY Course materials, Manchester University Press.

TASK ANALYSIS BASELINE RECORDING SHEET

Student ..*Alan*.. Trainee ..*Jacky*.................................
Target Behaviour..*Alan will tie his shoe laces with his shoe on the table.*............................
.... Criterion....*3/3*.....................................
Presentation..*"Alan, tie your shoe laces" (or similar)*......... Reward..*Praise*.............................

Steps No.		Description	Baseline Trials				
Init.	Rev.		1	2	3	4	5
1		Tie knot					
2		Pick up R lace with L hand and R hand and form loop					
3		Keep loop held with R hand and withdraw L hand					
4		Pick up L lace with L hand and wrap over the loop and over the fore finger					
5		Take L lace from over fore finger around fore fimger and out to front by thumb					
6		Place loop between middle and 3rd finger of L hand					
7		Put spare lace through the loop and pull through with fore finger and thumb of R hand					
8		Pull tight					
9							
10							

Score Guide: 4 - Correct / No help
3 - Good / Verbal prompt
2 - Better / Gestural prompt
1 - Some idea / Physical prompt
x - Incorrect. 0 - No response

Init. = Initial steps suggested from the task analysis
Rev. = Revised steps following baseline observations.

EDY Course materials, Manchester University Press.

TASK ANALYSIS BASELINE RECORDING SHEET

Student .... Trainee ....

Target Behaviour...

.... Criterion...

Presentation.. Reward...

Steps No.		Description	Baseline Trials				
Init.	Rev.		1	2	3	4	5
1							
2							
3							
4							
5							
6							
7							
8							
9							
10							

Score Guide: 4 - Correct / No help
3 - Good / Verbal prompt
2 - Better / Gestural prompt
1 - Some idea / Physical prompt
x - Incorrect.   0 - No response

Init. = Initial steps suggested from the task analysis
Rev. = Revised steps following baseline observations.

EDY Course materials, Manchester University Press.

BEHAVIOUR RECORD SHEET

UNIT: 5

Score Guide: 4 - Correct / No help, 3 - Good / Verbal prompt,
2 - Better / Gestural prompt, 1 - Some idea / Physical prompt,
x - Incorrect, 0 - No response.

VIDEO DEMONSTRATION: ADULTS

Target Behaviour *Alan will tie his shoe laces with shoe on the table.*

Criterion *3/3*

Presentation *"Alan tie your shoe laces" (or similar)* Reward *Praise*

T= *Jacky*
S= *Alan*

Step no.	Description	Trials														
		1	2	3	4	5	6	7	8	9	10	11	12	13	14	15
1	Pick up R lace + form loop															
2	L lace over loop + fore finger															
3	L lace round fore finger to thumb															

PRACTICE WITH STUDENT

Target Behaviour .... Criterion ....

Presentation .... Reward ....

T=
S=

Step no.	Description	Trials														
		1	2	3	4	5	6	7	8	9	10	11	12	13	14	15

VIDEO DEMONSTRATION: CHILDREN AND YOUNG PEOPLE

Target Behaviour *Sarika will load tape into 'Walkman', listen to it through headphones, teacher steadying the 'Walkman'.* Criterion *2/2*

Presentation *Sarika, can you play the tape" (or similar).* Reward *Praise and music*

T= *Barbara*
S= *Sarika*

Step no.	Description	Trials														
		1	2	3	4	5	6	7	8	9	10	11	12	13	14	15
1	Open lid															
2	Load tape															
2a	Push tape down															
2b	Slot tape in when handed it															

ROLE PLAY

Target Behaviour .... Criterion ....

Presentation .... Reward ....

T=
S=

Step no.	Description	Trials														
		1	2	3	4	5	6	7	8	9	10	11	12	13	14	15

S = Student   T = Trainee

EDY Course materials, Manchester University Press

TRAINEE ASSESSMENT FORM

UNIT: 5

Score Guide: 4 - Excellent, 3 - Good approximation,
2 - Approximately correct, 1 - Poor approximation,
x - Incorrect, 0 - Incorrect (no action), - - Irrelevent.

VIDEO DEMONSTRTION: ADULTS

Target Behaviour *Alan will tie his shoe laces with his shoe on the table.*

Criterion *3/3.*

Presentation *"Alan, tie your shoe laces". (or similar).* Reward *Praise.*

Trainee behaviour	Trials															Data Summary		
	1	2	3	4	5	6	7	8	9	10	11	12	13	14	15	No. of Trials	Score	%
Prepares Teaching																		
Presents Task																		
Prompts																		
Rewards																		

T = *Jacky*   S = *Alan*

PRACTICE WITH STUDENT

Target Behaviour ....

Presentation .... Criterion .... Reward ....

Trainee behaviour	Trials															Data Summary		
	1	2	3	4	5	6	7	8	9	10	11	12	13	14	15	No. of Trials	Score	%
Prepares Teaching																		
Presents Task																		
Prompts																		
Rewards																		

T =   S =

EDY Course Materials, Manchester University Press

VIDEO DEMONSTRATION: CHILDREN AND YOUNG PEOPLE

Target Behaviour *Sarika will load tape into "Walkman" . listen to it through headphones, teacher steadying "Walkman".*

Criterion *2/2*

Presentation *"Sarika, can you play the tape". (or similar).* Reward *Praise and music.*

Trainee behaviour	Trials															Data Summary		
	1	2	3	4	5	6	7	8	9	10	11	12	13	14	15	No. of Trials	Score	%
Prepares Teaching																		
Presents Task																		
Prompts																		
Rewards																		

T = *Barbara*   S = *Sarika*

ROLE PLAY

Target Behaviour ....

Presentation .... Criterion .... Reward ....

Trainee behaviour	Trials															Data Summary		
	1	2	3	4	5	6	7	8	9	10	11	12	13	14	15	No. of Trials	Score	%
Prepares Teaching																		
Presents Task																		
Prompts																		
Rewards																		

T =   S =

S = Student   T = Trainee

UNIT 6

Shaping

6.1 INTRODUCTION

Complex behaviours such as walking and talking are built up from simple forms. In the case of talking, for example, the normally developing child progresses from simple sounds and babble through two and three word sentences to adult forms of speech. Each stage of development can be regarded as an **approximation** to the final form. The method used to build up complex behaviours from simple forms is called **shaping.**

The term shaping takes its name from the art of the potter who starts with a shapeless lump of clay. Gradually the clay is shaped and moulded into the required form. During this process the clay is seen to take shape and at various stages during the activity clear approximations to the target can be recognised. When teaching, we shape up new behaviour by prompting and rewarding successive approximations to the target behaviour.

6.2 TASK ANALYSIS AND SUCCESSIVE APPROXIMATIONS

In the units on prompting and task analysis it was stressed that a complicated piece of behaviour must be analysed into small stages or steps. In the physical prompting example, the child was required to pick up a ring and locate it on a post. This was done in several steps. Initially the child was rewarded simply for letting go of the ring after it had been located on the post. The release of the ring, whilst not the full target behaviour, is nevertheless an approximation to it - it is the **first approximation** to the target behaviour.

Three steps or approximations to the target behaviour are shown below:
1st approximation: ring on the top of post; child lets go.
2nd approximation: ring near the top of post; child locates on to post and lets go.
3rd approximation: ring on table; child picks ring up takes it to post, locates it
                                 and lets go. This is the target behaviour.

It should be noted that each approximation includes the previous one. Thus the second approximation (locates on post), includes the first (lets go). In this way approximations are **successive**. Task analysis (the identification of essential steps) can be viewed as a means of determining the successive approximations on the way to the target behaviour. In this example, the last part of the task (lets go) was taught first. This is called **backward training**. On the kettle task in the task analysis unit, the first part of the task (fill the kettle) was taught first. This is called **forward training.**

FIGURE 6.1   **Shaping by <u>Forward Training</u>**

TARGET BEHAVIOUR: To eat with a spoon with minimum spilling

<u>1st approximation</u>
Pick up the spoon

<u>2nd approximation</u>
Pick up the spoon and load the food

<u>3rd approximation</u>
Pick up spoon, load food
and place in mouth

<u>4th approximation</u>
Pick up spoon, load food, place
in mouth and withdraw spoon

6.3 SHAPING BY FORWARD TRAINING

Target behaviour: to eat with a spoon with minimum spilling. In this example the person is required to pick up the spoon, load food onto it, place it in his or her mouth, take the food off the spoon and withdraw the spoon.

In Figure 6.1 the task has been analysed into four sequential steps in the natural order in which they occur:

1st approximation: pick up the spoon

FIGURE 6.2   Shaping by <u>Backward Training</u>

TARGET BEHAVIOUR: To eat with a spoon with minimum spilling

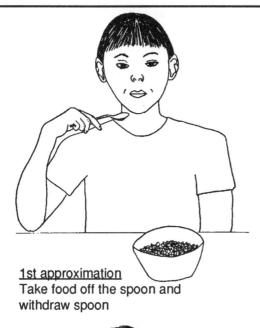

<u>1st approximation</u>
Take food off the spoon and
withdraw spoon

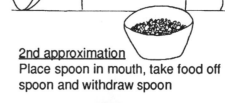

<u>2nd approximation</u>
Place spoon in mouth, take food off
spoon and withdraw spoon

<u>3rd approximation</u>
Load food onto spoon, place spoon in mouth,
take food off spoon and withdraw spoon

<u>4th approximation</u>
Pick up spoon, load food, place spoon in mouth,
take food off spoon and withdraw spoon

2nd approximation: pick up spoon and load the food
3rd approximation: pick up spoon, load food and place in mouth
4th approximation: pick up spoon, load food, place in mouth and take food off
                              spoon, withdraw spoon.

Each step or approximation incorporates the previous one. They are successive
approximations to the target behaviour.

6.4 SHAPING BY BACKWARD TRAINING

If we look at the four steps of the eating with spoon task again (Figure 6.1), it is clear that only Step 4 constitutes the target behaviour. Steps 1 - 3 do not result in the target behaviour. Thus the student only completes the whole task when at the end of training, that is, on the last step. If the order of teaching the steps were reversed, so that the last step was taught first, the student would always complete the task at every step of the teaching process. Re-analysing the task in reverse order gives the following steps - see Figure 6.2.

1st approximation :	take the food off the spoon, withdraw spoon from mouth.
2nd approximation :	place spoon in mouth, take food off spoon, withdraw spoon from mouth.
3rd approximation :	load food onto spoon, place in mouth, take food off spoon, withdraw spoon.
4th approximation :	pick up spoon, load food, place in mouth, take food off spoon, withdraw spoon.

In the above sequence the first step taught is the last part of the task. Similarly the second step taught is the second to last part of the task. This backward order of teaching the steps, starting with the last part of the task, is called **backward training.**

6.5 DECIDING WHEN TO USE FORWARD OR BACKWARD TRAINING

For people with severe learning difficulties backward training is frequently the preferred method of teaching. The advantage of backward training is that the student always completes the task after each trial. This means that the task as a whole should have more meaning and that the reward can be given at the natural point (i.e. for completion of the target) and not at an arbitrary point part way through (e.g. a reward for picking up the spoon). In the above example, starting by teaching the student to take the food off the spoon and withdraw the spoon carries with it the immediate reward of the food and is generally a more meaningful activity than picking up the spoon (the first step in the forward training sequence). Similarly when teaching a young child to assemble a constructional toy, teaching the last step first makes it easier to see how the completed toy will look and hence is likely to be more intrinsically rewarding. The first step may bear no resemblance to the completed toy and hence teaching it first may not be particularly rewarding and so extrinsic rewards will need to be strong in order to keep the child motivated.

However there are many tasks, e.g. learning to play a musical instrument, which are better taught through forward training. Suppose the target behaviour is for a person to play the tune "Happy Birthday" on the recorder. The teacher has to use a forward training procedure, the exact sequence of which would depend on the student's performance on a series of baseline trials.

Similarly, when teaching someone eye contact forward training has to be used. Suppose that the target behaviour is for the student to look at the teacher for three seconds. The teacher may start by attracting the student's attention by showing a reward, e.g. a small sweet, and giving it to the student when he or she looks at it. The sweet is then placed near to the teacher's eyes and the student receives the reward for looking at it in that position. The reward is then placed directly in line with the student's and the teacher's eyes and then moved to the side of the teacher's head. The reward is given only if the student's eyes remain focussed on the teacher's, if only for a split second or so at first.

Gradually the reward is moved further from the teacher's head and the length of time the student has to look at the teacher's eyes is increased before the reward is given. In this example a forward training procedure is used whereby the student is rewarded for making successive approximations to the target behaviour of giving eye contact for three seconds.

6.6 DECIDING WHETHER TO DEMONSTRATE AND/OR PROMPT THE WHOLE TASK ON EACH TRIAL

Having decided on the task analysis and on whether to use forward or backward training, the teacher then has to decide whether, during each trial, to demonstrate or to prompt those parts of the task on which the student is not yet working. In the example of tying shoe laces this can be done in the following way. Using backward training the first step to be taught might be "pull laces tight". The teacher would therefore carry out the earlier steps of tying a knot and making a bow and then ask the student to pull the laces tight. The teacher is thus giving a demonstration of the early steps in the sequence on every trial.

In the eating with spoon task, using backward training on Step 1 (taking food off spoon and withdrawing the spoon), it would be appropriate for the teacher to use hand over hand guidance (full physical prompt) to lead the student through picking up the spoon, loading it and placing it in the student's mouth and then release the student's hand to allow completion of the task. This would also apply if forward training was used on Step 1 (picking up the spoon) in that the student would first be asked to pick up the spoon and be rewarded for so doing. The teacher would then give physical prompting through the rest of the task.

Performing the whole of the task on each trial helps the student to understand how all the steps fit together. However for complicated tasks with many steps, each trial may take an extremely long time if the teacher performs or prompts all the steps on which the student is not yet working. This may result in the student spending too long passively watching and not enough time practising the part of the task that is being worked on. In this case, it is more profitable for the teacher to concentrate on teaching one step, hence keeping the trials short, and when this is mastered link it to the next step and so on until the student has mastered the whole task.

The above discussion does not apply to tasks which the teacher cannot demonstrate such as teaching eye contact.

6.7 SUMMARY

1   Complex behaviour is taught by first analysing the essential steps and then by rewarding successive approximations to the target behaviour. This is called **shaping**.
2   In **forward training** the first step is taught first and the student progresses forwards through the task.
3   In **backward training** the last step is taught first, then the second to last and so on until the student completes the whole task unaided.
4   Backward training is recommended for teaching many tasks as on every step the student completes the task and is rewarded at the natural point.

5   However there are several tasks, e.g. eye contact or learning a musical instrument, which can only be taught using forward training.
6   When teaching a task using forward or backward training, it is important to decide whether, on every trial, it is possible or desirable for the teacher to demonstrate those parts of the task on which the student is not yet working.

Please answer the study questions on this unit before starting the practical session.

STUDY QUESTIONS

1   Before teaching a task, we must break it down into its essential .... This is called ....
2   Each step of the task can be regarded as an .... to the Target Behaviour.
3   When a step of a task incorporates the previous one it is called a .... approximation.
4   Building complex behaviour from simpler forms is called ....
5   a) If we teach the steps of a task in the natural order in which they occur, we are using ....
     b) It is called this because the first step that is taught is the .... part of the task and the student moves progressively .... through the task.
6   a) If we teach the steps of a task in the reverse order to which they normally occur we are using ....
     b) It is called this because the first step that is taught is the .... part of the task and the student moves progressively .... through the task.
7   The advantage of .... is that at the end of each trial in the teaching process the student completes the task.

8   List three tasks which might be suitable to teach using backward training.
     a) ....
     b) ....
     c) ....

9   List three tasks which might be more suitable to teach using forward training.
     a) ....
     b) ....
     c) ....

PRACTICAL WORK

PREPARATION PRIOR TO PRACTICAL

The aim of the practical work on this unit is for you to choose a task, consider different ways in which it can be analysed, break it down into steps which are appropriate for the student you have chosen to work with and consider how these should be linked together in the teaching session. We strongly suggest that you practice using backward training on this unit particularly if you used forward training on Unit 5. Use the Session Planning Sheet to help you prepare.

As for Unit 5, the need to make a task analysis and carry out baselines will make this practical session too long unless the following preparatory work is done beforehand.

1   Select a student who is ready to work on a task which can be taught using backward training.
2   Write the target behaviour.
3   Write out a rough task analysis with the steps in the reverse order. Use the **Task Analysis Baseline Recording Sheet** (page 127).
4   Carry out some baseline trials with the student and record their progress on each step.

la <u>**VIDEO DEMONSTRATION (Children and Young People)**</u>

The Student:

Neil is seven years old. He is generally an even tempered and content child who is somewhat passive. It is sometimes difficult to motivate him to become involved in classroom activities.

Target Behaviour:

Neil will put on his right sock. Criterion of success 2/3 correct.

Task Analysis - Backward Training:- (see Task Analysis Baseline Recording Sheet)

    Step 1 Neil will pull his sock up to knee from his ankle.
    Step 2   ..   .. over his heel and up to his knee.
    Step 3   ..   .. from over his toes, over his heel and up to his knee.
    Step 4   ..   ..   put his sock over his toes, over the heel and up to his knee.

Recording:

Record Neil's progress on the BRS including the baseline trial. Watch the tape again and record the teacher's performance on the TAF. Use ALL categories if possible.

Comments:

Note the clear preparation and presentation of each trial. After trial 7 the teacher felt that the social reward was losing its strength and so she decided to pair this with a crisp in order to maintain Neil's interest in the task. Do you think this was appropriate? The teacher used backward training in this session. However, she did not go through the whole task on each trial before getting to the step where Neil was asked to complete it. Consider the advantages and disadvantages of teaching him in this way.

It may be more appropriate to teach dressing tasks in more natural situations, for example, changing for P.E. or getting up in the morning. What do you think?

la VIDEO TAPE DEMONSTRATION (Adults)

The Student:

Morley attends a special care day centre. He has good fine motor skills and has many basic skills in his repertoire. However he is difficult to motivate. He practices laying the table every day for lunch.

Target Behaviour:

Morley will lay one place setting of knife, fork, spoon and glass with a mat in place. Criterion of success 2/2.

Baselines:

On the first baseline Morley is asked to lay the table (step 4) without a demonstration. The baseline is then repeated with a demonstration and prompting.

Task Analysis:

There are four steps in this task analysis (see Task Analysis Baseline Recording Sheet). They are written in the order for backward training. This means that the last step (step 4) is the target behaviour. Teaching begins on Step 1 (put spoon in correct position when all other parts are in place).

Recording:

Score Morley's progress on the two baseline trials on the Task Analysis sheet. Then score his progress on each step on the BRS. Watch the tape again and score Danny's teaching on ALL TAF categories if possible.

Comments:

Morley has the physical skills to pick up and move the cutlery but he sometimes needs a slight touch on the hand to make a response. For scoring, we have counted this as a gestural prompt (i.e. score of 2). Did Morley reach criterion on Step 1 before Danny moved on to the next step? Is it really necessary to ask Morley for eye contact before presenting a trial? Reaching criterion on Step 2 is not shown in order to shorten the tape and still show a trial on Step 3. Notice how Danny sensitively withholds prompts long enough to give Morley a chance to respond and does not over-prompt.

As regards PRESENTS TASK, there are some trials on which Danny demonstrates the task incorrectly. He gains Moreley's attention and then removes the cutlery ready for the start of the trial. It is important to get the cuttlery ready as part of PREPARES and before gaining Moreley's attention. This problem is noticeable on trials 3,7,8 and 9.

II Role Play

1 Discuss the baseline you have prepared and make any final revisions to the steps.
2 Prepare the teaching materials and seating arrangements.
3 Teach on a trial by trial basis and record the student's progress on the BRS.
4 Your instructor will guide you through the session and record your progress on the TAF.

III Practice with child/adult

Teach the student using the same procedure as that used in Role Play.

IV Some issues to consider during feedback

1 Was backward or forward training appropriate for your task?
2 How will you teach the student to work on this and similar tasks in other settings and with different people?
3 What is the difference between Shaping and Task Analysis?

UNIT 6   SESSION PLANNING SHEET

NAME OF STUDENT

TARGET BEHAVIOUR

CRITERION OF SUCCESS

REWARDS TO BE USED

PRESENTATION (*i.e. verbal instruction to use, demonstration*)

METHOD OF TEACHING (*e.g. backward training, imitation*)

ANY OTHER DETAILS

TASK ANALYSIS BASELINE RECORDING SHEET

Student ...*Neil*.. Trainee ...*Farzana*..

Target Behaviour...*Neil will put on his right sock.*...

.... Criterion...*2/3*...

Presentation...*'Neil, can you put your sock on' (or similar)* Reward...*Praise*...................................

Steps No.		Description	Baseline Trials				
Init.	Rev.		1	2	3	4	5
1		*Pull sock up from ankle to knee.*					
2		*Pull sock up over heel and up to knee.*					
3		*Pull sock on from toes, over heel and up to knee.*					
4		*Put the sock on over toes + heel and up to knee.*					
5							
6							
7							
8							
9							
10							

Score Guide: 4 - Correct / No help

3 - Good / Verbal prompt

2 - Better / Gestural prompt

1 - Some idea / Physical prompt

x - Incorrect.   0 - No response

Init. = Initial steps suggested from the task analysis

Rev. = Revised steps following baseline observations.

EDY Course materials, Manchester University Press.

TASK ANALYSIS BASELINE RECORDING SHEET

Student ..... *Morley* .... Trainee ..... *Danny* ....

Target Behaviour. *Morley will lay one place setting of knife, fork, spoon and glass with a mat in place.*

.... Criterion.... *2/2* ....

Presentation.. *"Morley, can you lay the table"* .... Reward.... *Praise* ....

Steps No.		Description	Baseline Trials $\mathcal{D}$				
Init.	Rev.		1	2	3	4	5
1		*Place spoon in position (other items in place)*					
2		*Place fork and spoon in position (other items in place)*					
3		*Place knife, fork and spoon in position (other items in place)*					
4		*Place glass, knife, fork and spoon in position*					
5							
6							
7							
8							
9							
10							

Score Guide: 4 - Correct / No help $\mathcal{D} = Demonstration$

3 - Good / Verbal prompt

2 - Better / Gestural prompt

1 - Some idea / Physical prompt

x - Incorrect.   0 - No response

Init. = Initial steps suggested from the task analysis

Rev. = Revised steps following baseline observations.

EDY Course materials, Manchester University Press.

TASK ANALYSIS BASELINE RECORDING SHEET

Student .... Trainee ....

Target Behaviour...

.... Criterion...

Presentation.. Reward...

Steps No.		Description	Baseline Trials				
Init.	Rev.		1	2	3	4	5
1							
2							
3							
4							
5							
6							
7							
8							
9							
10							

Score Guide: 4 - Correct / No help

3 - Good / Verbal prompt

2 - Better / Gestural prompt

1 - Some idea / Physical prompt

x - Incorrect. 0 - No response

Init. = Initial steps suggested from the task analysis

Rev. = Revised steps following baseline observations.

EDY Course materials, Manchester University Press.

BEHAVIOUR RECORD SHEET   UNIT: 6

Score Guide: 4 - Correct / No help,   3 - Good / Verbal prompt,
2 - Better / Gestural prompt,   1 - Some idea / Physical prompt,
x - Incorrect,   0 - No response.

VIDEO DEMONSTRATION: CHILDREN AND YOUNG PEOPLE

Target Behaviour ..*Neil will put on his right sock*......
Criterion ....*2/3*........
Presentation ..*"Neil, can you put your sock on."*..(or similar). Reward ..*Praise (+ crisp from trial 8)*..

T= *Tarzana*
S= *Neil*

Step no.	Description	B	Trials															
		1	2	3	4	5	6	7	8	9	10	11	12	13	14	15		
1	Pull sock from ankle																	
2	Pull sock from heel																	
3	Pull sock from toe																	
4	Put on sock (TB)																	

VIDEO DEMONSTRATION: ADULTS

Target Behaviour ..*Morley will lay one place setting of knife, fork, spoon and glass with a mat in place.*.. Criterion ..*2/2*..
Presentation ..*"Morley, can you lay the table."*.. Reward ..*Praise*..

T= *Danny*
S= *Morley*

Step no.	Description	Trials														
		1	2	3	4	5	6	7	8	9	10	11	12	13	14	15
1	Lay spoon (other items in place)															
2	Fork + Sp (other items in place)															
3	Kn, Fo, +Sp (other items in place)															

ROLE PLAY

Target Behaviour .... Criterion ....Reward ....
Presentation ....

Step no.	Description	Trials														
		1	2	3	4	5	6	7	8	9	10	11	12	13	14	15

T=
S=

PRACTICE WITH STUDENT

Target Behaviour .... Criterion ....
Presentation ....Reward ....

Step no.	Description	Trials														
		1	2	3	4	5	6	7	8	9	10	11	12	13	14	15

T=
S=

S = Student   T = Trainee   B = Baseline

EDY Course materials, Manchester University Press

Score Guide: 4 - Excellent, 3 - Good approximation, 2 - Approximately correct, 1 - Poor approximation, x - Incorrect, 0 - Incorrect (no action), - - Irrelevant.

TRAINEE ASSESSMENT FORM   UNIT: 6

VIDEO DEMONSTRATION: CHILDREN AND YOUNG PEOPLE

<u>Target Behaviour</u> *Neil will put on his right sock.* Criterion *2/3*

Presentation *"Neil, can you put your sock on" (or similar)* Reward *Praise (+ crisp from trial 8)*

T= *Farzana*   S= *Neil*

Trainee behaviour	B	Trials															Data Summary		
	1	2	3	4	5	6	7	8	9	10	11	12	13	14	15		No. of Trials	Score	%
Prepares Teaching																			
Presents Task																			
Prompts																			
Rewards																			

VIDEO DEMONSTRTION: ADULTS

<u>Target Behaviour</u> *Morley will lay one place setting of knife, fork, spoon and glass with a mat in place.* Criterion *2/2*

Presentation *"Morley, can you lay the table"* Reward *Praise*

T= *Danny*   S= *Morley*

Trainee behaviour	Trials															Data Summary		
	1	2	3	4	5	6	7	8	9	10	11	12	13	14	15	No. of Trials	Score	%
Prepares Teaching																		
Presents Task																		
Prompts																		
Rewards																		

PRACTICE WITH STUDENT

<u>Target Behaviour</u> .... Criterion ....

Presentation .... Reward ....

T=   S=

Trainee behaviour	Trials															Data Summary		
	1	2	3	4	5	6	7	8	9	10	11	12	13	14	15	No. of Trials	Score	%
Prepares Teaching																		
Presents Task																		
Prompts																		
Rewards																		

ROLE PLAY

<u>Target Behaviour</u> .... Criterion ....

Presentation .... Reward ....

T=   S=

Trainee behaviour	Trials															Data Summary		
	1	2	3	4	5	6	7	8	9	10	11	12	13	14	15	No. of Trials	Score	%
Prepares Teaching																		
Presents Task																		
Prompts																		
Rewards																		

S = Student   T = Trainee   B = Baseline

EDY Course Materials, Manchester University Press

UNIT 7

Imitation

7.1 IMITATION AND LEARNING

We say that a person imitates when he or she copies the behaviour of others. The ability to imitate develops from early infancy. The young baby first learns to imitate his or her own behaviour - repeating simple actions such as arm waving or sounds. This is gradually extended so that, for example, a young child might discover that waving his or her arm produces an interesting noise or movement because a mobile has been accidentally hit. At first the child may not associate the action of waving with the effect caused, but the reinforcement of noise and movement will lead to repetition, i.e. the child learns the association. Eventually the child will make efforts to reproduce the effect by deliberately trying to knock the mobile. The child is now in effect attempting to imitate his or her own actions. Similarly with sounds, a baby may discover a new speech sound and attempt to repeat it, for example "dada....dada". Many early behaviours emerge in this way through self imitation. This process is also reinforced by others rewarding the child's self imitating behaviour.

Soon we may try to develop the child's repertoire of behaviours further by providing alternative **models** to imitate. Indeed much of our behaviour is shaped in this way, particularly language. Imitation is used with young children to teach a wide variety of skills, using games such as "This is the way we clap our hands", or "Pat-a-cake, pat-a-cake baker's man". As children develop further, they learn to imitate complex sequences of behaviour, e.g. bathing a doll in the same way that they are bathed by their parents.

As so much of our learning depends on our ability to imitate others, it is important that we help people with severe learning difficulties to develop this skill. Indeed there is evidence to suggest that people with learning difficulties have particular problems in learning how to imitate. Imitation provides the means whereby we can learn new skills. If a person can copy someone's behaviour (i.e. imitate), then an important tool with which to learn new behaviours has been acquired.

In this unit we will be considering the teaching of imitation to people who do not imitate or who are just acquiring this skill. In imitation training the teacher demonstrates, i.e. provides a **model**, which the student has to imitate.

7.2 TYPES OF MODEL

There are two types of model: **gestures** (actions) and **speech sounds** (including words).

Gestures. In order to respond to a model the student must attend to it. In the case of gesture we would gain the student's attention by saying "look" or calling his or her name. When the student is attending, the model (the gesture or action that should be imitated) is presented with the words "do this". If the student imitates or makes an approximation to the model a reward is given immediately. If you are teaching Makaton, for example, you would present the action and the word together as the model, followed by saying "do this" or "you do it".

Sounds and words. To teach sound imitation, a similar pattern is followed. The sound model is announced by the word "say........." followed by the sound/word to be imitated, for example "say.......... book".

7.3 SHAPING IMITATION

Pre-requisites for imitation. It is sometimes tempting to try to teach someone to imitate without checking that he or she is able to learn in this way. For the student to imitate he or she must be aware of the presence of another person and realise that the behaviour being demonstrated by the teacher should be copied. If it is possible to engage the student in eye contact, if he or she can take part in reciprocal games, e.g. rolling a ball back and forth with another person, then there is a good chance that teaching using imitation will be successful.

Where to start. Teaching should begin with actions already familiar to the student, that is familiar gestures or sounds. Unless there is severe motor impairment, simple arm or hand movements should be the easiest to imitate, such as shake a tambourine, tap on the table, clap hands, hands on knees.

Establishing the imitation game. Initially the student is required to imitate one familiar gestural model (e.g. folding arms). A second model is then introduced involving another gesture familiar to the student (e.g. clap hands). Once the student reliably responds to both models, presented at random, we can be sure that he or she is discriminating between them and focussing directly on the gestures to be imitated. The "game" of imitation is now established in that the student knows that in this teaching session imitation will be required and the teacher can now introduce new and more complex models.

Successive approximations through forward training. In teaching a new response through imitation training it is necessary to reward any approximation to the model. In the case of teaching clap hands, this may simply be raising both hands at first. Gradually the student's responses would be shaped, by prompting, until the hands are moved together and before finally being clapped. In the case of speech sound imitation, any movements of the lips or any sound should be accepted as the first approximation.

Accentuating the model. Many gestures and all sounds disappear after presentation as a model. The student in this case has to reproduce the model from memory. If in some way the model can be retained, then the student can produce the imitation at the same time as the model, making the task easier. For instance, with a gesture like waving "bye bye", the teacher can carry on waving while prompting the student with the other hand. It is more difficult to retain a sound model, but some attempt can be made by frequently repeating the sound, for example "say ball...ball...ball...," allowing the student a few seconds to respond following each repetition.

If the model is a gesture, then it can be exaggerated or accentuated by increasing the range of movement of the action. For example in the case of clapping hands, the teacher could start with the arms stretched out to the side and bring them together in a wide sweeping movement. If the model is a sound, then it can be accentuated by saying it loudly or by opening the mouth wider, and so on.

7.4 THE AIM OF IMITATION TRAINING

People can learn through imitation provided the teacher models (i.e. **demonstrates)** what is required and the student understands that he or she is to copy the model. However many people with severe learning difficulties have difficulty in learning to imitate in the first place. Hence the initial aim of imitation training is to teach the student to learn from (i.e. copy) the behaviour of others. Viewed in this way imitation is a "learning to learn" skill. When the student can imitate, a whole range of new behaviours can be taught. As the student reliably imitates new models, they can be faded so that the student will eventually perform independently.

7.5 THE APPLICATION OF IMITATION TRAINING

The functional use of objects. Objects are typically associated with the way they are used. Hence a cup is associated with drinking, a spoon with eating or stirring, shoes with putting on our feet. When teaching a young child to discriminate between objects we usually model the social function of the object. For instance we build with bricks, we push a toy car or we cuddle a doll. By **imitating** our actions the young child can learn how to use objects appropriately. The ability to make distinctions between objects by using them appropriately is an important stage towards developing the ability to name them, either verbally or non-verbally.

Non verbal communication. People without speech often develop alternative ways of communicating their needs. For example, a person may pull on the teacher's arm to indicate an object or actually prompt the teacher to perform a desired activity. This is sometimes referred to as "means-end" behaviour in that the person has discovered the means (pulling the teacher's arm) to get the ends (the desired object). Means-end behaviour of this sort may be viewed as pre-requisites for shaping gestures into non-verbal signs expressing needs. Instead of pulling the teacher towards an object, the student could be taught, through imitation, to point to the desired object. This could be extended by teaching the student to imitate a simple sign, taken from a standard sign language, to represent the desired object. Consistent pairing of speech with such signs should improve verbal understanding as well as increase speech production.

Perceptual-motor, self-help and cognitive tasks. There is tremendous scope for the application of imitation training in all these areas. For example, teaching someone how to thread a needle, butter toast, read unfamiliar words and many more. In each of these examples the teacher first models the correct response and the student imitates.

7.6 SUMMARY

1   Imitation is an important skill normally acquired in infancy.
2   People with learning difficulties may need to be taught to imitate other people's behaviour in order to make use of imitation as a "learning to learn" skill.
3   Once a person can imitate, new behaviours can be taught by rewarding **successive approximations** to the model.
4   In the early stages of learning to imitate a new model, it helps if the teacher **accentuates** the model and (except in sound imitation) **physically prompts** the student.
5   Imitation can be used as a way of teaching verbal or non verbal communication as well as perceptual-motor, self-help and cognitive tasks.
6   By fading models, independent behaviours can be promoted.

Please answer the study questions on this unit before starting the practical session.

STUDY QUESTIONS

1   In many teaching situations the student acquires new skills by .... the demonstration given by the teacher.

2   When we demonstrate the task to the student, we have provided a ....

3   The two types of model used in imitation training are .... and ....

4   It is essential to get the student's .... before presenting the model.

5   If the student fails to imitate parts of the model we can improve the model by
     a) ....
     b) ....

6   The student should be .... for attempting to imitate a new model even if the imitation is only approximate.

7   Once the student can reliably imitate the model, it can be .... to encourage independent behaviour.

8   List three contrasting skills which can be taught using imitation training.
     a) ....
     b) ....
     c) ....

PRACTICAL WORK

The aim of the practical work on this unit is for you to practice imitation training, either teaching someone who is only just learning how to imitate to copy simple movements, or teaching someone who can make simple imitations to extend their range of imitative behaviour. Use the session planning sheet to help you prepare (page 139).

la VIDEO TAPE DEMONSTRATION (Children and Young People)

The Child:

Alan is nine years old. Generally he is a passive child who has a very pleasant personality and is usually co-operative in class. At present he has no spoken language.

Target Behaviour:

Alan will imitate the following Makaton signs : "book", "cup", "car" and "plate". Criterion of success 2/2 for each sign.

Recording:

Record Alan's progress on the BRS. Start after he has imitated "clap hands" and "stamp feet". Watch the tape again and record the teacher's performance on the TAF, using ALL categories.

Comments:

Note how the teacher first establishes the game of imitation by asking Alan to imitate relatively straightforward actions - clap hands and stamp feet. Alan has only recently started to learn these Makaton signs. Therefore, at this stage, the teacher rewards his **attempts** to make the correct sign for each object.

Think of ways in which teaching sign imitation can be generalised to other less structured settings. How could Alan learn to use these signs independently?

lb VIDEO DEMONSTRATION (Adults)

The Student:

Jacky has cerebral palsy but is able to move her arms and can clap her hands and wave. However she does not yet make these actions in imitation of a model. Jacky is very sociable and enjoys contact from others.

Target Behaviour:

Jacky will imitate the two gross motor actions of wave hand and clap hands. Criterion of success 2/2 for each action.

Recording:

Record Jacky's progress on the BRS. Note that the BRS scoring system can be used to record approximations to a target behaviour as well as or instead of the amount of prompting. For example, compare Jacky's score on trial 3 with her score on trials 1 and 2. Watch the tape again and record Angie's teaching on ALL TAF categories.

Comments:

Although it is quite difficult to gain Jacky's attention, Angie does manage to do this by calling her name and by waiting for her to turn and look at her. Jacky shows that she may just be ready to begin imitating in as much as she begins to lift one arm for the wave sign and two for the clap hands (approximations to the targets). There is a long way to go yet however. Note the really positive social reward used by Angie.

II ROLE PLAY

1   Almost any task can be taught through imitation.   However for this unit we suggest that you either: a) choose someone who is only just learning **how** to imitate and teach straightforward gross motor actions e.g. clapping hands, hands on knees; or b) choose someone who can already imitate and teach sign or sound imitation.
2   Write the target behaviour. In particular be absolutely clear how precisely you require the student to imitate.   You could use a shaping procedure and reward successive approximations to the target behaviour.
3   Prepare the seating arrangements and materials. Remember it is almost always necessary to sit opposite the student when teaching imitation in order to ensure that eye contact is gained at the start of each trial.
4   Teach on a trial by trial basis and record progress on the BRS.
5   Your instructor will guide you through the session and record your performance on the TAF.

III PRACTICE WITH STUDENT

Teach the student using the same procedure as that used in Role Play.

IV   SOME ISSUES TO CONSIDER DURING FEEDBACK

1   When presenting a model it is absolutely essential for the student to attend closely. Did you have any problems with this?
2   Did you manage to keep up with your recording? This can be a problem in imitation training as the time taken to complete a trial is often very short.
3   Think of tasks that can be taught using imitation in less structured settings.

UNIT 7   SESSION PLANNING SHEET

NAME OF STUDENT

TARGET BEHAVIOUR

CRITERION OF SUCCESS

REWARDS TO BE USED

PRESENTATION (i.e. verbal instruction to use, demonstration)

METHOD OF TEACHING (e.g. backward training, imitation)

ANY OTHER DETAILS

BEHAVIOUR RECORD SHEET

UNIT: 7

Score Guide: 4 - Correct / No help, 3 - Good / Verbal prompt,
2 - Better / Gestural prompt, 1 - Some idea / Physical prompt,
x - Incorrect, 0 - No response.

VIDEO DEMONSTRATION: ADULTS

Target Behaviour *Jacky will imitate two gross motor actions of 'wave' and 'clap hands'.*
.... Criterion *2/2 for each action*
Presentation *"Jacky, you do it": Angie waves or claps.* Reward *Praise* ....

S= *Jacky* T= *Angie*	Step no.	Description	Trials															
			1	2	3	4	5	6	7	8	9	10	11	12	13	14	15
	1	Imitate 'wave'																
	2	Imitate 'clap hands'																

PRACTICE WITH STUDENT

Target Behaviour .... Criterion ....
Presentation .... Reward ....

S=	Step no.	Description	Trials															
T=			1	2	3	4	5	6	7	8	9	10	11	12	13	14	15

VIDEO DEMONSTRATION: CHILDREN AND YOUNG PEOPLE

Target Behaviour *Alan will imitate the Makaton signs for 'book', 'cup', 'car' and 'plate'.*
.... Criterion *2/2 for each sign.*
Presentation *"Alan, do this": Brit shows sign and says word* Reward *Praise* ....

S= *Alan* T= *Brit*	Step no.	Description	Trials															
			1	2	3	4	5	6	7	8	9	10	11	12	13	14	15
	1	Imitate 'book'																
	2	Imitate 'cup'																
	3	Imitate 'car'																
	4	Imitate 'plate'																

ROLE PLAY

Target Behaviour .... Criterion ....
Presentation .... Reward ....

S=	Step no.	Description	Trials															
T=			1	2	3	4	5	6	7	8	9	10	11	12	13	14	15

S = Student   T = Trainee

EDY Course materials, Manchester University Press

Score Guide: 4 - Excellent, 3 - Good approximation,
2 - Approximately correct, 1 - Poor approximation,
x - Incorrect, 0 - Incorrect (no action), - - Irrelevent.

TRAINEE ASSESSMENT FORM   UNIT: 7

VIDEO DEMONSTRATION: CHILDREN AND YOUNG PEOPLE

Target Behaviour *Alan will imitate the Makaton signs for 'book', 'cup', 'car' and 'plate'.*
Criterion *2/2 for each sign.*
Presentation *"Alan, do this": Brit shows sign and says word.* Reward *Praise*

Trainee behaviour	Trials															Data Summary		
	1	2	3	4	5	6	7	8	9	10	11	12	13	14	15	No. of Trials	Score	%
Prepares Teaching																		
Presents Task																		
Prompts																		
Rewards																		

T= *Brit*   S= *Alan*

VIDEO DEMONSTRTION: ADULTS

Target Behaviour *Jacky will imitate two gross motor actions of 'wave' and 'clap hands'.*
Criterion *2/2 for each action*
Presentation *"Jacky, you do it": Angie waves or claps.* Reward *Praise*

Trainee behaviour	Trials															Data Summary		
	1	2	3	4	5	6	7	8	9	10	11	12	13	14	15	No. of Trials	Score	%
Prepares Teaching																		
Presents Task																		
Prompts																		
Rewards																		

T= *Angie*   S= *Jacky*

ROLE PLAY

Target Behaviour ....
Presentation .... Criterion .... Reward ....

Trainee behaviour	Trials															Data Summary		
	1	2	3	4	5	6	7	8	9	10	11	12	13	14	15	No. of Trials	Score	%
Prepares Teaching																		
Presents Task																		
Prompts																		
Rewards																		

T=   S=

PRACTICE WITH STUDENT

Target Behaviour ....
Presentation .... Criterion .... Reward ....

Trainee behaviour	Trials															Data Summary		
	1	2	3	4	5	6	7	8	9	10	11	12	13	14	15	No. of Trials	Score	%
Prepares Teaching																		
Presents Task																		
Prompts																		
Rewards																		

T=   S=

S = Student   T = Trainee

EDY Course Materials, Manchester University Press

UNIT 8

Putting it all Together

READING ASSIGNMENT

8.1 INTRODUCTION

Behavioural teaching techniques, as featured on the EDY course, are not unique to teaching people with severe learning difficulties. Task analysis, prompting, reinforcement and so on feature in a great deal of our learning, often without our realizing it. However for people with severe learning difficulties the systematic application of behavioural methods provides an effective means whereby we can teach a great many new skills. The aim of Phase I of the EDY course has been to provide training in how to apply these techniques successfully in one to one teaching.

Up to now each unit has dealt with a specific behavioural teaching technique which you have practised under the guidance of your instructor. In each session you will also have practiced techniques covered on other units. Therefore by now you will have a feel for how the techniques can be integrated in a teaching situation.

In this short reading assignment the main points covered on each unit are summarized. In the practical work you will be responsible for planning and carrying out a teaching session with minimum help from your instructor. His or her role will be to observe your performance using the TAF on which you will need to score 75% or over in order to qualify for a certificate.

8.2 THE EDY UNITS

Unit 1 **Antecedents and Setting Conditions.** All our behaviour is affected by the environment in which we live and work - the setting conditions. As this environment is forever changing, there will be times when people may want to work and other times when they may not. As teachers it is important that we are aware of how the setting conditions might be affecting the behaviour of those we are trying to teach. We should try to create the most favourable setting conditions and control the antecedents - the specific task we ask someone to do - so that learning is most likely to take place.

Unit 2 **Planning Individual Teaching.** When deciding what to teach, we need to set clear target behaviours. Teaching new skills should be done on a trial by trial basis, starting with a few baseline trials. A trial consists of, a) preparing the student and task, b) presenting the task, c) prompting, d) the student's response and e) rewarding. The student's progress on each trial should be recorded.

Unit 3   **Using Rewards.** Learning is more enjoyable and motivating if we are rewarded for our efforts. Sometimes it is not easy to find out what is rewarding for a person with severe learning difficulties and we may need to carry out a reward assessment. Pairing known rewards, e.g. a drink, with an unknown reward like praise, helps the student to begin to associate praise with something pleasant and hence it will eventually become a reward in itself. Using rewards effectively encourages learning. Rewards should be given immediately, enthusiastically and consistently.

Unit 4   **Prompting.** This is a set of techniques which the teacher can use to help the student through a difficult part of the task. There are physical, gestural and verbal prompts. It is important to reward trials where the student has to be prompted. As the student becomes more proficient, prompts can be faded from greatest to least assistance so that eventually the student performs unaided.

Unit 5   **Task Analysis.** For people with severe learning difficulties even the simplest task may be very complicated and hence it will need to be broken down into small steps. In this way the student can be taught in a step by step way until the whole task is mastered.

Unit 6   **Shaping.** In a shaping procedure we reward successive approximations to the target behaviour. To do this we may use forward or backward training. For many tasks backward training is an effective method as each trial always ends with the target behaviour completed. This helps the student to see how the whole task fits together.

Unit 7   **Imitation.** In imitation training the student initially has to learn to copy, i.e. imitate, what the teacher has done. Many people with severe learning difficulties have particular problems in learning how to imitate. Accentuating the model to be imitated, exaggerating or retaining it, helps the student to perform the imitation task. Once the student can imitate reliably, a great many new tasks can be taught using this technique.

8.4 SUMMARY

When planning and carrying out individual teaching sessions with people who have severe learning difficulties you should be able to:

1   Set clear target behaviours.
2   Write task analyses which are appropriate for the student and the task.
3   Carry out baseline trials and amend the task analysis accordingly.
4   Teach on a trial by trial basis.
5   Prompt sensitively, using the minimum help necessary for the person to learn.
6   Use the appropriate shaping technique, forward or backward training.
7   Use clear models for the student to imitate.

8   Use rewards that make learning enjoyable and encourage learning.

9   Record the student's progress on each trial.

There are no study questions on this unit. However you should complete the EDY quiz after the end of the practical session.

PRACTICAL WORK

The aim of this unit is for you to plan and carry out a teaching session using the behavioural techniques that have been covered on this course. You will receive minimum help from your instructor whose main role is to record you performance on the TAF on which you should score 75% or over in order to qualify for a certificate.

I VIDEO DEMONSTRATION

There is no video demonstration for this unit.

II PREPARATION PRIOR TO SESSION

Before the session, spend some time planning as follows using the session planning sheet (page 151).

1   Choose a student who is co-operative.
2   Select a task which he or she is ready to learn.
3   Write the target behaviour. Specify the materials you will use and the criterion of success.
4   Write out the task analysis on the Task Analysis Baseline Recording Sheet (page 153).
5   Carry out some baseline trials and revise the task analysis accordingly.
6   Decide on the criterion of success for each step.
7   Decide whether to use forward or backward training.
8   Prepare the BRS using the full size version. (Spare sheets are in the back of this workbook).
8   Think about how you may need to prompt the student.
9   Decide on the rewards you are going to use.
10   Consider how important it will be for the student to imitate all or parts of the task in order for learning to occur.
11   Practice teaching a few trials.

III ROLE PLAY

Role Play should be carried out in the usual way although your instructor will only take the part of the student. If two trainees are taking the course, you can each take the part of teacher and student with the instructor taking an observational role.

IV PRACTICE WITH STUDENT

Teach the student using the same procedure as that used in Role Play. Aim to complete 20 trials. During the teaching session the instructor will record your performance on the TAF. You will receive feedback at the end of the session and your recording sheets will be collected.

V SOME ISSUES TO CONSIDER DURING FEEDBACK

1 Which aspects of the behavioural approach to teaching have you found easy to use? Which have caused you problems?
2 Are there specific groups of people with severe learning difficulties for whom this approach is particularly suited? Are there some for whom it is less suited?
3 Can the EDY approach be applied in all areas of teaching or are there some for which it is more applicable than others?

At the end of this session you should complete the EDY quiz that you first filled in at the start of the course. Your instructor will give you feedback on your answers in due course. Remember you need to obtain a score of 50% or over to qualify for a certificate.

UNIT 8   SESSION PLANNING SHEET

NAME OF STUDENT

TARGET BEHAVIOUR

CRITERION OF SUCCESS

REWARDS TO BE USED

PRESENTATION *(i.e. verbal instruction to use, demonstration)*

METHOD OF TEACHING *(e.g. backward training, imitation)*

ANY OTHER DETAILS

TASK ANALYSIS BASELINE RECORDING SHEET

Student .... Trainee ....

Target Behaviour..

.... Criterion...

Presentation.. Reward..

Steps No.		Description	Baseline Trials				
Init.	Rev.		1	2	3	4	5
1							
2							
3							
4							
5							
6							
7							
8							
9							
10							

Score Guide: 4 - Correct / No help
3 - Good / Verbal prompt
2 - Better / Gestural prompt
1 - Some idea / Physical prompt
x - Incorrect. 0 - No response

Init. = Initial steps suggested from the task analysis
Rev. = Revised steps following baseline observations.

EDY Course materials, Manchester University Press.

BEHAVIOUR RECORD SHEET (BRS)

Target Behaviour..................

....

Criterion..................

Presentation..................

Reward..................

Score Guide: 4 - Correct / No help
3 - Good / Verbal prompt
2 - Better / Gestural prompt
1 - Some idea / Physical prompt
x - Incorrect. 0 - No response

Step no.	Description	1	2	3	4	5	6	7	8	9	10	11	12	13	14	15	16	17	18	19	20
																					T
																					S

Trials

=T

=S

S = Student   T = Trainee

EDY Course materials, Manchester University Press.

PHASE II

APPLYING EDY IN CONTEXT

INTRODUCTION

Congratulations on successfully completing Phase I of the EDY Course! As you know the main emphasis during Phase I was helping you to improve your individual teaching techniques when working with people who have severe learning difficulties. The training format involving video, role play and practice with student was intended to provide the optimum conditions for you to improve these techniques. Phase II is a vital part of the EDY course as it provides an opportunity to integrate the behavioural teaching approach into your daily work.

To complete Phase II you should:

a) Go through the reading assignments in Parts A and B.
b) Plan an individual teaching programme for someone with whom you work regularly.
c) Discuss the programme with your instructor and with any other trainees who are also working on Phase II.
d) Teach the programme in the normal work environment up to 5 times a week over a four week period. (The instructor should observe at least two of your teaching sessions).
e) Consider the way in which your setting is organised to maximise students' participation and learning and discuss ways of making improvements.

The written section of Phase II is in two parts, A and B. Part A contains guidelines on planning and teaching your individual programme. Part B discusses the rationale behind room management and asks you to consider ways in which the organisation of your setting could be improved. Each part contains a short reading assignment and suggests some key points to discuss at a meeting with your instructor.

Although there is no structured format for completing Phase II you will need to hold at least 3 meetings with your instructor to complete this Phase of the EDY course successfully. The purpose of these meetings is as follows.

Meeting 1:   Discuss the overall aims of Phase II, consider a student and task for your teaching programme, confirm dates for future meetings.

             (Before the next meeting you should read Part A and complete the Phase II planning sheets).

Meeting 2:   Discuss your teaching programme and make arrangements for the instructor to observe you teaching it.

             (Before the next meeting you should read Part B on room management).

Meeting 3:   Review the progress of you teaching programme. Discuss the room management scheme in your setting.

Normally there should be a week between the first two meetings and about three weeks between meetings 2 and 3. However your instructor will give you guidance about the exact number and timing of meetings.

PART A: PLANNING AND IMPLEMENTING A TEACHING PROGRAMME

1.1 PRELIMINARY READING

From Acquisition to Generalisation

During Phase I of the course you practised using behavioural teaching techniques under the guidance of your instructor. These are summarized in Unit 8. In this part of Phase II you will use these techniques to plan a programme and teach it to someone with whom you work regularly. This programme should be related to the student's overall needs. Your instructor will give you guidance throughout, and will observe you working on the programme so that you can receive immediate feedback.

As mentioned in the introduction to Phase I, EDY techniques are most applicable when teaching people with severe learning difficulties to learn new and unfamiliar tasks. This is sometimes referred to as the **acquisition** stage of learning (Haring et al, 1981). At this stage the student generally needs the maximum help from the teacher in order to reach the target behaviour. As the student becomes more competent the teacher's direct role in teaching reduces. The student is then encouraged to perform the skill independently, in different settings and with different materials. It is only when the student can reliably generalise the skill in this way that it has been truly learned.

This process by which learning occurs can be illustrated by reminding ourselves of the example of someone learning to drive a car which was referred to in the introduction to Phase I of the course. Initially the learner will need a great deal of help from the driving instructor as the complexities of learning to drive are grappled with (acquisition stage of learning). Gradually driving becomes more automatic and the learner is eventually able to drive any car in an increasingly varied set of weather and traffic conditions (generalisation stage of learning). Only now has the learner become a fully competent driver. Indeed this stage of competence is almost always reached well after the learner has passed the driving test.

Units 1 to 7 of Phase I of the EDY course are similar to the acquisition stage of learning in that you practised using behavioural, techniques under the guidance of your instructor. In Unit 8 you planned the teaching session with less help and hence began to move into the generalisation phase of learning. Phase II represents a continuation of this process as you will plan a teaching programme and implement it in your usual work setting.

There is therefore a parallel between the process of going through Phase I of the EDY course and that of teaching a new skilll to someone who has severe learning difficulties:- both represent the acquisition stage of learning. As students become more competent in the skill that has been taught and can perform it independently, they have moved into the generalisation stage in the same way that you will do as you integrate behavioural teaching techniques such as EDY into your daily work.

Planning Your Programme

It is important for your Phase II programme to dovetail into a complete individual programme plan (IPP). The IPP should be broad, balanced and relevant to the student's overall needs. It will hopefully have been planned by all those involved in working with the student including, if possible, the student as well. Fagg et al (1990) provide examples of children's programmes of work which illustrate how this can be done.

The following is a list of points to consider when planning your Phase II programme.

1   What is the student's overall programme plan?
2   Were you involved in planning it?
3   Is it going well?
4   How will you decide on the target behaviour for your Phase II programme?
     e.g. i)   its relevance to the overall teaching plan
          ii) whether the student wants to learn this task
          iii) whether it is achievable
5   Where will you teach the programme?
6   How frequently?
7   Are there factors in your setting which might help or hinder you?
7   Will anybody else share the teaching, e.g. parent, co-worker?
8   How will you plan for generalisation?

Do not choose a target behaviour for your Phase II programme simply because it will be easy to teach using EDY techniques

The Phase II planning sheets (see below) are designed to help you plan your programme. The first one has been completed on someone for whom a Phase II programme has already been planned. This is intended as a model to help you plan your own programme. Complete the Phase II planning sheet and Task Analysis Baseline Recording Sheet on someone with whom you will work during Phase II. An additional sheet is provided should you change your mind about the programme following discussion with your instructor.

1.2 MEETING WITH INSTRUCTOR

Discuss your completed Phase II planning sheet with your instructor and make adjustments where necessary. Although Behaviour Record Sheets (BRS) are provided in the workbook, the setting in which you work may be using different forms. Provided you and your instructor consider that these are appropriate for recording the student's progress on your Phase II programme, then there is no reason why you should not use them. The EDY recording sheets were never intended to be the only ones that could be used when teaching people with severe learning difficulties.

Following this meeting you should be able to run the programme in your work setting with support from your instructor.

*   Start by revising the task analysis if necessary and conduct further baseline trials.
*   Decide on the rewards you will use.
*   Will you use forward or backward training?

* Prepare your recording sheets.
* Have the necessary materials and equipment to hand
* Make sure you have a regular time and place to work with the student and that other staff memebers are aware of this.
* Teach the programme every day if possible and record each trial. Short, regular and frequent sessions are more likely to be successful than infrequent, irregular and longer ones.

Progress will be reviewed in subsequent meetings with your instructor during Phase II.

PHASE II PLANNING SHEET

NAME OF STUDENT   *Steven   (age 6)*

TARGET BEHAVIOUR   *Steven will copy his first name correctly.*

CRITERION OF SUCCESS   *4/4 on five consecutive teaching sessions*

REWARDS   *Praise*

PRESENTATION (i.e. verbal instruction to use, demonstration)
"Steven, can you copy your name" (or similar)

METHOD OF TEACHING (e.g. backward training, imitation)
Backward training

TEACHING ARRANGEMENTS
Where will you teach ?   *In the class individual teaching area*

When will you teach?   *Three or four times a week, 5 minutes per session*

	Tick if this applies
WHY CHOOSE THIS TARGET BEHAVIOUR?	
It is central to the overall programme plan	✓
The student's parents would like this skill to be taught	✓
The student would like to learn this task	✓
It is achievable	✓
The necessary materials and equipment are available	✓
You will have enough time to teach it	✓

Other reasons :

Name writing is part of a whole class early literacy programme.

HOW WILL YOU TEACH THE STUDENT TO GENERALISE THIS SKILL?

1 By teaching Steven to write his name independently, without copying.
2 By teaching him to recognise and copy his name written in different scripts - e.g. italics, capital letters.
3 By asking him to write his name on his pictures, birthday cards etc.

ANY OTHER DETAILS
Steven is cheerful and cooperative in the classroom. He enjoys 1 to 1 teaching but needs to be encouraged to join in more with the other children.

TASK ANALYSIS BASELINE RECORDING SHEET

Student ..... *Steven* ..... Trainee ..... *Joanne* .....
Target Behaviour..... *Steven will copy his first name correctly* .....
..... Criterion.. *4/4 on five consecutive sessions* .....
Presentation.. *'Steven, can you copy your name'* ..... Reward... *Praise* .....

Steps No.		Description N.B. On _all_ steps he is presented with a clear model of 'Steven' for him to copy.		Baseline Trials				
Init.	Rev.			1	2	3	4	5
1		Overwrites	*S t e v e n*					
2		Overwrites and completes	*S t e v e _*					
3		' ' '	*S t e v _ _*					
4		' ' '	*S t e _ _ _*					
5		' ' '	*S t _ _ _ _*					
6		' ' '	*S _ _ _ _ _*					
7		Copies 'Steven'	*_ _ _ _ _ _*					
8		Copies 'Steven' (no 'dashes')						
9								
10								

Score Guide: 4 - Correct / No help
3 - Good / Verbal prompt
2 - Better / Gestural prompt
1 - Some idea / Physical prompt
x - Incorrect.   0 - No response

Init. = Initial steps suggested from the task analysis
Rev. = Revised steps following baseline observations.

EDY Course materials, Manchester University Press.

PHASE II PLANNING SHEET

NAME OF STUDENT

TARGET BEHAVIOUR

CRITERION OF SUCCESS

REWARDS

PRESENTATION (i.e. verbal instruction to use, demonstration)

METHOD OF TEACHING (e.g. backward training, imitation)

TEACHING ARRANGEMENTS

   Where will you teach ?

   When will you teach?

	Tick if this applies
WHY CHOOSE THIS TARGET BEHAVIOUR?	
It is central to the overall programme plan	-
The student's parents would like this skill to be taught	-
The student would like to learn this task	-
It is achievable	-
The necessary materials and equipment are available	-
You will have enough time to teach it	-

   Other reasons :

HOW WILL YOU TEACH THE STUDENT TO GENERALISE THIS SKILL?

ANY OTHER DETAILS

TASK ANALYSIS BASELINE RECORDING SHEET

Student .... Trainee ....
Target Behaviour...
.... Criterion...
Presentation... Reward...

Steps No.		Description	Baseline Trials				
Init.	Rev.		1	2	3	4	5
1							
2							
3							
4							
5							
6							
7							
8							
9							
10							

Score Guide: 4 - Correct / No help
3 - Good / Verbal prompt
2 - Better / Gestural prompt
1 - Some idea / Physical prompt
x - Incorrect.   0 - No response

Init. = Initial steps suggested from the task analysis
Rev. = Revised steps following baseline observations.

EDY Course materials, Manchester University Press.

TASK ANALYSIS BASELINE RECORDING SHEET

Student .... Trainee ....

Target Behaviour...

.... Criterion...

Presentation.. Reward...

Steps No.		Description	Baseline Trials				
Init.	Rev.		1	2	3	4	5
1							
2							
3							
4							
5							
6							
7							
8							
9							
10							

Score Guide: 4 - Correct / No help
3 - Good / Verbal prompt
2 - Better / Gestural prompt
1 - Some idea / Physical prompt
x - Incorrect.   0 - No response

Init. = Initial steps suggested from the task analysis
Rev. = Revised steps following baseline observations.

EDY Course materials, Manchester University Press.

PART B: ROOM MANAGEMENT

2.2 PRELIMINARY READING

Rationale for Room Management

Individual teaching, the main focus of the EDY course so far, does not take place in isolation. No matter how well planned and appropriate a teaching programme may be, it will not be successful unless the **context** in which the teaching occurs is carefully planned.

The aim of this section is to see how individual teaching can be incorporated into the total range of activities that are provided for children and adults with severe learning difficulties in whatever setting they live and work. Room management procedures provide a way of organizing the environment so that this can occur.

Room management (see Thomas, 1985; McBrien and Weightman, 1980, and Porterfield et al, 1977) was initially developed as a means of organising staff time so that one staff member could keep a group of people with severe learning difficulties busy whilst allowing another to do individual work. Staff were given prescribed roles for specific intensive periods of the day to enable this to occur. The following breakdown of staff roles was typical of many schemes.

Individual worker: teaches the individual programmes.

Room manager: has a series of rapid contacts with the remainder of the group keeping them busy by prompting those who are not attending to tasks and by rewarding those who are.

Mover: deals with visitors to the room, provides materials for the manager and, if time, does some individual work.

Early research showed that this approach increased the amount of individual teaching which took place and that the "on task" behaviour of those in the group was much higher than when they were in non room management conditions.

The overall rationale for room management has now been extended to include the following additional features.

a) The term 'Room Management' now refers to the allocation of staff roles throughout the <u>whole time</u> that they are responsible for working with people with severe learning difficulties. This could be in the work centre and/or in a variety of community settings.

b) Room management should enable individual teaching to take place in the most appropriate context and with relevant materials.

c) Successful room management allows group members to be engaged in a variety of useful activities <u>all of which</u> should be related to each person's individual programme plan. It is not sufficient for group members simply to be kept busy working on activities which may be of no relevance to them.

d)   Room management therefore helps students to generalise their learning by
         working independently with less direct help from their teachers.

Therefore in schools, day centres, homes and other settings where people with severe
learning difficulties live and work, it is important for the management of the whole day to
be organised so that all students are involved in meaningful activities. A balance between
direct teaching, group activities, leisure etc is essential if we are to ensure that each
person's programme is sufficiently broad, balanced and relevant to meet his or her
individually assessed needs. Room management procedures provide a way of organizing
the work setting so that this balance can be achieved - (see Brown and Brown ,1987,
and Mansell et al,1987, for a discussion of some of the issues.

Factors affecting the implementation of specific room management schemes.

Room management can therefore be adapted to any setting. However individual
schemes vary greatly from setting to setting and depend on a variety of factors.

First, the ratio of staff to students in the setting. Room management schemes reflect the
staff/student ratio that exits in a particular setting. With ratios of 20 students to 2 staff,
that may exist in a day centre attended by adults, it is difficult for the staff to work as
intensively with groups or individuals on a broad range of activities than is possible with
ratios of 10 students to 3 staff which are often found in special schools.   This is one of
the main reasons why the quality of education and care is typically considered better for
children than it is for adults.

Second, the availability of relevant materials and equipment. Successful room
management depends a great deal on there being enough suitable and readily available
equipment for everybody to work with which is matched to the students abilities and
interests. Not surprisingly people get bored and the activities may be of little educational
value if a limited range is available.

Third, the relationships between the staff are crucial. This is perhaps the key to successful
room management. By definition room management involves staff working together
both in planning and operating the scheme. Hence it is vitally important for the staff to
get on well with each other. Resentments, misunderstandings, etc, will inevitably affect
the success of the scheme.

The above are just a few of the factors which can affect the way in which a specific room
management scheme is adopted in a particular setting. Ultimately those responsible for
planning the room management scheme, having taken account of the above and other
factors, arrive at a compromise so that the best possible system can be put into action
given the constraints which operate.

Hence there is no one way to plan successful room management. Each setting has its
own unique features which determine the most appropriate procedure to use. The
example in Figure 1 shows how one scheme can work.

FIGURE 1

NURSERY TIMETABLE - STAFF ROLES   Summer Term Week 6

		MORNING		AFTERNOON
MON	INDIVIDUAL GROUP ROOM SPLASH ROOM	*Maria* *Joanne* *Doreen* *Sue*	LOWER SCHOOL MUSIC	COMPUTER — *Doreen* SOFT ROOM — *Joanne*
TUES	INDIVIDUAL GROUP ROOM COMPUTER	*Doreen* *Maria* *Michelle* *Joanne*	INDIVIDUAL — *Maria* ROOM — *Michelle* COMPUTER — *Joanne* SOFT ROOM — *Doreen*	LEISURE
WED	INDIVIDUAL GROUP ROOM	*Joanne* *Michelle* *Doreen / Maria*	HYDROTHERAPY — *Doreen / Joanne* *Jackie / Michelle* INDIVIDUAL — *Maria* GROUP	HOME ECONOMICS — *Doreen* SHOPPING — *Joanne / Maria*
THURS	INDIVIDUAL GROUP ROOM	*Joanne* *Doreen* *Maria*	INDIVIDUAL — *Doreen* LIBRARY — *Maria* GROUP — *Joanne*	SWIMMING — *Joanne / Maria* SOFT ROOM — *Doreen / Mary*
FRI	INDIVIDUAL GROUP ROOM SPLASH ROOM	*Maria* *Joanne* *Doreen* *Sue*	INDIVIDUAL — *Doreen* GROUP — *Maria* LIBRARY — *Joanne*	GROUP DANCING — *Maria* SOFT ROOM — *Doreen* SINGING — *Joanne* *Michelle*

INDIVIDUAL = Individual worker
GROUP = Group worker
ROOM = "Mover"

SPLASH and SOFT ROOMS are areas of the school where students can engage in water play and gross motor activities with a member of staff.
LEISURE is a time when all students in the junior department choose from a range of leisure activities.

**Some observations about the Room Management scheme in the Nursery class.
(See Figure 1)**

1   This class contains 18 children aged between 2 and 5 years, 9 of whom have severe
    learning difficulties and 9 are "play group" children.

2   Staff numbers vary between 3 and 4, one is the class teacher and the others are
    nursery nurses.

3   The timetable is planned at a weekly meeting of the four staff when their roles are
    allocated.

4   In Figure 1:
    "Individual" refers to the member of staff who does individual work;
    "Group" refers to the person who works with a small group on a topic.
    "Room" refers to the staff member who deals with interruptions, toilets the children
    and, if time, helps the group worker.
    "Splash" and "soft room" are areas in the school where small groups of children can
    engage in water play and gross motor games respectively.
    In the "Leisure" afternoon the children in the whole junior department can choose
    a particular activity and they may work in another class or with different staff.
    The remainder of the activities are self explanatory.

5   Individual teaching takes place in the morning and is restricted to the 9 children with
    severe learning difficulties.

6   The staff keep a record of how much individual teaching each child has on each of
    their programmes.

7   Each child's programme also contains aims and objectives for group work and out
    of class activities.

8   The timetable indicates how much class time is given to out of class activities e.g.
    music with the whole junior department, swimming, "soft" and "splash" rooms,
    dance, shopping, home economics, library.

9   At times during the week the group divides. For example on Wednesday afternoon
    some go shopping while others do home economics.

2.2 MEETING WITH INSTRUCTOR.

1 Bring details of the room management scheme or other organisational sysyem which
   operates in your setting if you have one and any other documents that you think would
   be relevant.

2 Discuss your scheme in detail, paying particular attention to the factors referred to in
   the preliminary reading above.

3 Consider the strengths of your scheme and ways in which it could be improved.

4 How does your work on your Phase II programme fit into this scheme?

5 Discuss the progress of your Phase II programme.

BIBLIOGRAPHY

Ackerman, D. and Mount, H. (l99l) *Literacy for All.* London: Fulton.

Aherne, P. and Thornber, A. (l990) *Mathematics for All.* London: Fulton.

Aherne, P. and Thornber, A. (l990) Communication for All. London: Fulton.

Ashdown, R., Carpenter, B. and Bovair , K. (Eds) (l99l) *The Curriculum Challenge: Access to the National Curriculum for Pupils with Severe Learning Difficulties.* London: Falmer Press.

Bishop, J. (1989) *An evaluation of an EDY course for parents of childen with severe learning difficulties.* Unpublished MEd dissertation, University of Manchester.

Brown, H. and Brown, V. (1987) *Bringing People Back Home: Participation in Every Day Activities.* Bexhill on Sea: Outset Publishing.

Coupe, J., Barton, L., Barber, M., Collins, I., Levy, D. and Murphy, D. (1985) *The Affective Communication Assessment.* Manchester Education Committee, (available from SERIS, Westwood Street, Manchester, M14).

Fagg, S. Aherne, P., Skelton, S. and Thornber, A. (l990) *Entitlement for All in Practice: A Broad, Balanced and Relevant Curriculum for Pupils with Severe and Complex Learning Difficulties in the l990s.* London: Fulton.

Fagg, S. and Skelton, S. (l990) *Science for All.* London: Fulton.

Farrell, P. (1982) An evaluation of an EDY course in behaviour modification techniques for teachers and care staff in an ESN(S) school. *Special Education Forward Trends,* 9, 21-25.

Farrell, P. and Sugden, M. (1984) An Evaluation of an EDY Course in a School for Children with Severe Learning Difficulties. *Educational Psychology.* 4, 185-198.

Farrell, P. (Ed) (1985) *EDY: Its Impact on Staff Training in Mental Handicap.* Manchester University Press.

Felce, D., Jenkins, J., de Kock, U. and Mansel, J. (1986) *The Bereweeke Skill-Teaching System (Adult Version).* NFER-Nelson, Windsor.

Flynn, M. (l988) *Independent Living for Adults with Mental Handicap.* London: Cassell.

Foxen,T. and McBrien, J. (1981) *Training Staff in Behavioural Methods: Trainee Workbook.* Manchester University Press.

Haring, N.G. Liberty, K.A. and White, O.R. (1981) *An investigation of phases of learning and facilitating instructional events for the severely/profoundly handicapped (final project report).* Seattle: University of Washington College of Education.

Her Majesty's Inspectorate (l985) *Better Schools.* London: HMSO.

Hogg. J., Foxen, T. and McBrien, J. (1977) *Training Staff Responsible for Profoundly Retarded Multiply Handicapped Children: An Application of Kiernan and Riddick's Behaviour Modification Staff Training Programme.* Hester Adrian Research Centre.

Kiernan, C.C. and Riddick, B. (1973) *A Programme for Training in Operant Techniques, Volume 1: Theoretical Units.* London: Thomas Coram Research Unit, University of London Institute of Education.

Kiernan, c. (l99l) Professional Ethics: Behaviour Analysis and Normalisation. In Remington, R. (Ed) *The Challenge of Severe Mental Handicap: A Behaviour Analytic Approach.* Chichester: Wiley.

McBrien, J. (1982) *An Evaluation of a Training Course in Behavioural Techniques for Staff Working with Severely Mentally Handicapped Children.* Unpublished B.P.S. Dip. Clin. Psych. Dissertation.

McBrien, J. (1985) Behavioural training for nurses in mental handicap: an application of the EDY Course. *Journal of Advanced Nursing,* 10, 337-343.

McBrien, J. and Weightman, J. (1980) The effect of Room Management procedures on the engagement of profoundly retarded children. *British Journal of Mental Subnormality,* 26, 1, 38-46.

McBrien, J. and Foxen, T. (1981) *Training Staff in Behavioural Methods: Instructor's Handbook.* Manchester University Press.

McBrien, J. and Edmunds, M. (1985) Evaluation of an EDY course for staff working with severely mentally handicapped children. *Behavioural Psychotherapy,* 13, 202-217.

McBrien, J and Felce, D. (in press) *Challenging Behaviour in People with Severe or Profound Learning Disabilities : A practical Handbook on the Behavioural Aproach.* BIMH Publications.

Mansell, J., Felce, D., Jenkins, J., deKock, V. and Toogood, S. (1987) *Developing Staffed Housing for People with Mental Handicaps.* Costello.

Mount, H. and Ackerman, D. (l99l) *Technology for All.* London: Fulton.

National Curriculum Council (l99l) *The National Curriculum and Pupils with Severe Learning Difficulties; Curriculum Guidance.* York: NCC.

National Curriculum Development Team - SLD. (1990) *Talking Point Number 2.* Cambridge Institute of Education.

O'Brien, J. (1987) A guide to lifestyle planning: using the Activities Catalogue to integrate services and natural support systems. In B. W. Wilcox and G. T. Bellamy (Eds) *The Activities Catalogue: An Alternative Curriculum for Youth and Adults with Severe Disabilities.* Brookes: Baltimore.

Remington , R. (l99l) (Ed) *The Challenge of Severe Mental Handicap: A Behaviour Analytic Approach.* Chichester, Wiley.

Robson (1981) A mini course in structured teaching. *British Journal of Special Education,* 8, 26-27.

Robson, C. (1988) Evaluating the Education of the Developmentally Yoyng (EDY) course for training staff in behavioural methods. *European Journal of Special Needs Education,* 3, 1, 13-32.

Sebba, J. (1988) *The Education of People with Profound and Multiple Handicaps.* Manchester University Press.

Sebba, J. and Fergusson, A. (1991) Reducing the Marginalisation of Pupils with Severe Learning Difficulties. In M. Ainscow (Ed), *Effective Schools for All.* London: Fulton.

Sebba, J. and Byers, R. (1992) The National Curriculum: control or liberation for children with learning difficulties. *The Curriculum Journal* 3, 1.

White, M. and Cameron, R.J. (1986) *Portage Early Education Programme.* NFER-Nelson

Wolfensburger, W. (l983) 'Social role valorisation': a proposed new term for the principle of normalisation. *Mental Retardation,* 2l. 234-239.

ANSWERS TO STUDY QUESTIONS FOR EACH UNIT ON PHASE I

Unit 1

1 Setting conditions, antecedents and consequences,
2 E.g. A (i) At work reading reports,
   (ii) Telephone rings,
   (iii) Answer it,
   (iv) Have a useful discussion with the caller.
  E.g. B (i) Driving home after work,
   (ii) Traffic lights just about to turn red,
   (iii) Stop the car,
   (iv) Wait for the lights to change to green.
3 E.g. B (i) Driving home after work <u>one hour late</u>,
   (ii) Traffic lights about to turn red,
   (iii)Press accelerator and go through the red light,
   (iv) Arrive home a few seconds sooner.
4   i) Place, ii) Time, c) People, d) Personal.
5 a) Generalizing, b) discriminating.
   E.g. a) Using the toilet at school but not at home.
     b) Hugging everybody no matter who or where they are.

Unit 2

1 a) The Target Behaviour
  b) Exactly/precisely, i) observable verb, ii) the conditions in which the
    student should perform the task, and iii) the criterion of success.
2 E.g. John should catch the number 24 bus at 9.00am outside his house, pay for
  his ticket, get off at the stop near the day centre and arrive there at approximately
  9.20am every working day.
3 Baseline.
4 Trials.
5 End all pre-trial activity. Clear instruction.
6 Record.

Unit 3

1 E.g. a) Money, b) praise, c) food.
2 E.g. a) Watching T.V. "Soaps", b) playing football, c) gardening.
3 a) By getting to know the person well, b) multiple choice
  c) sequential sampling.
4 a) Immediately, b) enthusiastically, c) consistently.
5 Target behaviour
6 Easy
7 Difficult
8 Easy rewards: praise, cuddle
  Difficult rewards: sweet, music.
9 Pairing, "after".

Unit 4

1 Physical.
2 Gestural.
3 Verbal.
4 Fading.
5 Reducing, less.
6 Physical, gestural, verbal.
7 Verbal.
8 Reward, learn.
9 Teaching someone to steer a boat with a tiller.

Unit 5

1 Task Analysis.
2 Difficult.
3 a) Target behaviour, b) Steps, c) Baseline trials, d) Task Analysis.
4 Reached the criterion of success on the previous step.
6 a) Check that each trial is clearly presented and that the student is attending,
   b) Go back to the previous step to check that the reward is still working,
   c) Change the reward.
   d) If the student still has problems, do more task analysis.

Unit 6

1 Steps. Task Analysis.
2 Approximation.
3 Successive.
4 Shaping.
5 a) Forward Training, b)First, forward.
6 a) Backward Training, b) Last, backwards.
7 Backward Training.
8 E.g. a) putting on a jumper, b) using a public telephone,
        c) putting a letter in an envelope.
9 E.g. a) coin recognition, b) finding out what's on T.V.
        c) walking upstairs.

Unit 7

1 Imitating.
2 Model.
3 Gestural, verbal.
4 Attention
5 a) exaggerating it, b) retaining it.
6 Rewarded.
7 Faded.
8 E.g. a) sign language, b) speech sounds, c) laying the table.

APPENDIX   I

Spare Recording Sheets

Behaviour Record Sheets (BRS)

Trainee Assessment Forms (TAF)

Task Analysis Baseline Recording
Sheets (TABRS)

BEHAVIOUR RECORD SHEET (BRS)

Target Behaviour...

....

Criterion...

Presentation...

Reward..

Score Guide: 4 - Correct / No help
              3 - Good / Verbal prompt
              2 - Better / Gestural prompt
              1 - Some idea / Physical prompt
              x - Incorrect. 0 - No response

Trials

Step no.	Description	1	2	3	4	5	6	7	8	9	10	11	12	13	14	15	16	17	18	19	20

T=

S=

S = Student   T = Trainee

EDY Course materials, Manchester University Press.

BEHAVIOUR RECORD SHEET (BRS)

Target Behaviour..................................

Score Guide:
4 - Correct / No help
3 - Good / Verbal prompt
2 - Better / Gestural prompt
1 - Some idea / Physical prompt
x - Incorrect. 0 - No response

Criterion...
Presentation..
Reward..

Step no.	Description	Trials																			
		1	2	3	4	5	6	7	8	9	10	11	12	13	14	15	16	17	18	19	20

=T

=S

S = Student   T = Trainee

EDY Course materials, Manchester University Press.

BEHAVIOUR RECORD SHEET (BRS)

Target Behaviour...

....

Criterion...

Presentation...

Reward...

Score Guide: 4 - Correct / No help
3 - Good / Verbal prompt
2 - Better / Gestural prompt
1 - Some idea / Physical prompt
x - Incorrect.   0 - No response

Trials

Step no.	Description	1	2	3	4	5	6	7	8	9	10	11	12	13	14	15	16	17	18	19	20

T=

S=

S = Student   T = Trainee

EDY Course materials, Manchester University Press.

BEHAVIOUR RECORD SHEET (BRS)

Target Behaviour................................

....

Criterion................................

Presentation................................

Reward................................

Score Guide: 4 - Correct / No help
3 - Good / Verbal prompt
2 - Better / Gestural prompt
1 - Some idea / Physical prompt
x - Incorrect.   0 - No response

Trials

Step no.	Description	1	2	3	4	5	6	7	8	9	10	11	12	13	14	15	16	17	18	19	20

T=

S=

S = Student   T = Trainee

EDY Course materials, Manchester University Press.

TRAINEE ASSESSMENT FORM

Target Behaviour..................................

....

Criterion..

Presentation..

Reward..

Steps: 1..................................

2..................................

3..................................

4..................................

5..................................

Score Guide: 4 - Excellent
3 - Good approx
2 - Approx correct
1 - Poor approx

x - Incorrect
0 - Incorrect (no action)
- - Irrelevant

Rating Categories	Baseline/steps Trials																				Data Summary		
	1	2	3	4	5	6	7	8	9	10	11	12	13	14	15	16	17	18	19	20	No. of Trials	Score	%
Prepares Teaching																							
Presents Task																							
Prompts																							
Student's response																							
Rewards																							

S=

T=

S = Student   T = Trainee

EDY Course materials, Manchester University Press.

TRAINEE ASSESSMENT FORM

Target Behaviour..............

....

Criterion.........................

Presentation.....................

Reward...........................

Steps: 1...........................

2...........................

3...........................

4...........................

5...........................

Score Guide: 4 - Excellent

3 - Good approx

2 - Approx correct

1 - Poor approx

x - Incorrect

0 - Incorrect (no action)

- - Irrelevant

Rating Categories	Baseline/steps Trials																				Data Summary		
	1	2	3	4	5	6	7	8	9	10	11	12	13	14	15	16	17	18	19	20	No. of Trials	Score	%
Prepares Teaching																							
Presents Task																							
Prompts																							
Student's response																							
Rewards																							

S=

T=

S = Student   T = Trainee

EDY Course materials, Manchester University Press.

TRAINEE ASSESSMENT FORM

Target Behaviour...................................

....

Criterion...

Presentation..

Reward..

Steps: 1..

2..

3..

4..

5..

Score Guide: 4 - Excellent

3 - Good approx

2 - Approx correct

1 - Poor approx

x - Incorrect

0 - Incorrect (no action)

- - Irrelevant

Rating Categories	Baseline/steps Trials																				Data Summary		
	1	2	3	4	5	6	7	8	9	10	11	12	13	14	15	16	17	18	19	20	No. of Trials	Score	%
Prepares Teaching																							
Presents Task																							
Prompts																							
Student's response																							
Rewards																							

S=

T=

S = Student   T = Trainee

EDY Course materials, Manchester University Press.

TRAINEE ASSESSMENT FORM

Target Behaviour....................

Criterion.............................
Presentation.........................
Reward...............................

Steps: 1..........................
2..........................
3..........................
4..........................
5..........................

Score Guide: 4 - Excellent   x - Incorrect
3 - Good approx   0 - Incorrect (no action)
2 - Approx correct   - - Irrelevant
1 - Poor approx

Rating Categories	Baseline/steps Trials																					Data Summary		
	1	2	3	4	5	6	7	8	9	10	11	12	13	14	15	16	17	18	19	20	No. of Trials	Score	%
Prepares Teaching																							
Presents Task																							
Prompts																							
Student's response																							
Rewards																							

S=

T=

S = Student   T = Trainee

EDY Course materials, Manchester University Press.

TRAINEE ASSESSMENT FORM

Target Behaviour......................

....

Criterion..............................

Presentation..........................

Reward.................................

Score Guide: 4 - Excellent

3 - Good approx

2 - Approx correct

1 - Poor approx

x - Incorrect

0 - Incorrect (no action)

- - Irrelevant

Rating Categories	Baseline/steps																				Data Summary		
	Trials																				No. of Trials	Score	%
	1	2	3	4	5	6	7	8	9	10	11	12	13	14	15	16	17	18	19	20			
Prepares Teaching																							
Presents Task																							
Prompts																							
Student's response																					/////	/////	/////
Rewards																							

S=

T=

S = Student   T = Trainee

EDY Course materials, Manchester University Press.

TRAINEE ASSESSMENT FORM

Target Behaviour..................................

Steps:
1......................
2......................
3......................
4......................
5......................

Score Guide:
4 - Excellent
3 - Good approx
2 - Approx correct
1 - Poor approx

x - Incorrect
0 - Incorrect (no action)
- - Irrelevant

Criterion..................................

Presentation..................................

Reward..................................

Rating Categories	Baseline/steps Trials																				Data Summary		
	1	2	3	4	5	6	7	8	9	10	11	12	13	14	15	16	17	18	19	20	No. of Trials	Score	%
Prepares Teaching																							
Presents Task																							
Prompts																							
Student's response																							
Rewards																							

S=

T=

S = Student   T = Trainee

EDY Course materials, Manchester University Press.

TRAINEE ASSESSMENT FORM

Target Behaviour..........

Criterion..........

Presentation..........

Reward..........

Steps: 1..........

2..........

3..........

4..........

5..........

Score Guide: 4 - Excellent
3 - Good approx
2 - Approx correct
1 - Poor approx

x - Incorrect
0 - Incorrect (no action)
- - Irrelevant

Rating Categories	Baseline/steps Trials																				Data Summary		
	1	2	3	4	5	6	7	8	9	10	11	12	13	14	15	16	17	18	19	20	No. of Trials	Score	%
Prepares Teaching																							
Presents Task																							
Prompts																							
Student's response																							
Rewards																							

S=

T=

S = Student   T = Trainee

EDY Course materials, Manchester University Press.

TRAINEE ASSESSMENT FORM

Target Behaviour..................................

Steps: 1.................................

Criterion..................................

2.................................

3.................................

Presentation..................................

4.................................

Reward..................................

5.................................

Score Guide:
- 4 - Excellent
- 3 - Good approx
- 2 - Approx correct
- 1 - Poor approx

- x - Incorrect
- 0 - Incorrect (no action)
- -- Irrelevant

Rating Categories	Baseline/steps																					Data Summary		
	Trials																					No. of Trials	Score	%
	1	2	3	4	5	6	7	8	9	10	11	12	13	14	15	16	17	18	19	20			
Prepares Teaching																							
Presents Task																							
Prompts																							
Student's response																							
Rewards																							

S=

T=

S = Student   T = Trainee

EDY Course materials, Manchester University Press.

TASK ANALYSIS BASELINE RECORDING SHEET

Student .... Trainee ....
Target Behaviour..
.... Criterion...
Presentation.................................... Reward..

Steps No.		Description	Baseline Trials				
Init.	Rev.		1	2	3	4	5
1							
2							
3							
4							
5							
6							
7							
8							
9							
10							

Score Guide: 4 - Correct / No help
3 - Good / Verbal prompt
2 - Better / Gestural prompt
1 - Some idea / Physical prompt
x - Incorrect. 0 - No response

Init. = Initial steps suggested from the task analysis
Rev. = Revised steps following baseline observations.

EDY Course materials, Manchester University Press.

TASK ANALYSIS BASELINE RECORDING SHEET

Student .... Trainee ....
Target Behaviour...
.... Criterion...
Presentation... Reward..

Steps No. Init.	Rev.	Description	Baseline Trials 1	2	3	4	5
1							
2							
3							
4							
5							
6							
7							
8							
9							
10							

Score Guide: 4 - Correct / No help
3 - Good / Verbal prompt
2 - Better / Gestural prompt
1 - Some idea / Physical prompt
x - Incorrect. 0 - No response

Init. = Initial steps suggested from the task analysis
Rev. = Revised steps following baseline observations.

EDY Course materials, Manchester University Press.

TASK ANALYSIS BASELINE RECORDING SHEET

Student .... Trainee ....

Target Behaviour...

.... Criterion...

Presentation... Reward...

Steps No.		Description	Baseline Trials				
Init.	Rev.		1	2	3	4	5
1							
2							
3							
4							
5							
6							
7							
8							
9							
10							

Score Guide: 4 - Correct / No help
3 - Good / Verbal prompt
2 - Better / Gestural prompt
1 - Some idea / Physical prompt
x - Incorrect.   0 - No response

Init. = Initial steps suggested from the task analysis
Rev. = Revised steps following baseline observations.

EDY Course materials, Manchester University Press.

TASK ANALYSIS BASELINE RECORDING SHEET

Student .... Trainee ....

Target Behaviour...

.... Criterion...

Presentation.. Reward...

Steps No.		Description	Baseline Trials				
Init.	Rev.		1	2	3	4	5
1							
2							
3							
4							
5							
6							
7							
8							
9							
10							

Score Guide: 4 - Correct / No help

3 - Good / Verbal prompt

2 - Better / Gestural prompt

1 - Some idea / Physical prompt

x - Incorrect. 0 - No response

Init. = Initial steps suggested from the task analysis

Rev. = Revised steps following baseline observations.

EDY Course materials, Manchester University Press.

APPENDIX   II

Evaluation Materials   (for the course instructor)

EDY Quiz (A and B)

EDY Phase I Evaluation

EDY Phase I Course Summary Sheet

EDY Phase I Request for Certificate Form.

EDY QUIZ (A)

To be completed <u>before</u> you start Phase I of the course.

Name ....

1   Behaviour does not occur in isolation. It is influenced by the
    .... ,   the .... and the
    ....

2   What do we mean by the term "target behaviour"? ....
    ....

3   The written description of a target behaviour should include
    a) ....   b) ....
    c) ....

4   Before we start to teach a new task we should carry out a ....

5   Why is it important to use rewards in our teaching?
    ....

6   When you give a reward, you should present it in the following ways:
    a) ....
    b) ....
    c) ....

7   What is meant by the term prompting? ....
    ....

8   How is a prompt faded? ....

9   Breaking down a task into small steps is called ....

10 Why is it helpful to do this? ....
    ....

11 What should we do if the student is having difficulty in learning a step?

a) ....

b) ....

c) ....

d) ....

12 When should you move on to the next step in a teaching programme?

....

13 Teaching a task by starting on the last step is called

....

14 Teaching by rewarding successive approximations to the target behaviour
is called ....

15 The gesture or sound presented in imitation training is called a ....

16 If the student does not imitate the model you have presented, it can be
made easier either by .... the model
and/or by .... it.

EDY QUIZ (B)

To be completed <u>after</u> you have finished Phase I of the course.

Name ....

1 Behaviour does not occur in isolation. It is influenced by the
   .... , the .... and the
   ....

2 What do we mean by the term "target behaviour"? ....
   ....

3 The written description of a target behaviour should include
   a) ....   b) ....
   c) ....

4 Before we start to teach a new task we should carry out a ....

5 Why is it important to use rewards in our teaching?
   ....

6 When you give a reward, you should present it in the following ways:
   a) ....
   b) ....
   c) ....

7 What is meant by the term prompting? ....
   ....

8 How is a prompt faded? ....

9 Breaking down a task into small steps is called ....

10 Why is it helpful to do this? ....
    ....

11 What should we do if the student is having difficulty in learning a step?

a) ....

b) ....

c) ....

d) ....

12 When should you move on to the next step in a teaching programme?

....

13 Teaching a task by starting on the last step is called

....

14 Teaching by rewarding successive approximations to the target behaviour
is called ....

15 The gesture or sound presented in imitation training is called a ....

16 If the student does not imitate the model you have presented, it can be
made easier either by .... the model
and/or by .... it.

EDY PHASE I: EVALUATION

1. Please rank on a five point scale your views about the following aspects of Phase I of the EDY course, (5 = very useful, 1 = not at all useful).

	1	2	3	4	5	Brief Comments
Reading Assignments						
Video						
Role Play						
Practice with Student						

2. Which Units did you find the most useful?

3. Which Units could have been improved?

4. What did you like/find most useful about the course as a whole?

5. What suggestions would you make for improving it?

6. Any other comments.

Signed ....(Trainee)

EDY PHASE 1:   COURSE SUMMARY SHEET

INSTRUCTOR'S NAME (please print) ....

ADDRESS ....

....

STATUS OF INSTRUCTOR (e.g. teacher, officer in charge, nurse trainer, *Psychologist*)

LOCATION OF THE COURSE.

NAMES OF TRAINEES	STATUS	PLACE OF WORK
1 2 3 4 5 6 7 8		

COURSE STRUCTURE

Number of trainees per session

Frequency of sessions

Length of sessions

Number of trainees per instructor
in a session

NAMES OF CO -INSTRUCTORS (if any)	STATUS
1	
2	
3	

Please return this form, together with the <u>Request for Certificate Form</u>, to the Centre for Educational Guidance and Special Needs, University of Manchester, Oxford Road, Manchester, M13 9PL.
Please mark the envelope "EDY DATA".

EDY PHASE I: REQUEST FOR CERTIFICATE

TRAINEE'S NAME (as it should appear on the certificate, **PLEASE PRINT**)

STATUS OF TRAINEE (e.g. teacher, day care worker, nursery nurse, residential worker)

PLACE OF WORK (name, address and type of setting e.g. school, day centre, resedential home)

DATES OF THE COURSE (start and finish)

How many Units did the trainee attend sessions on?	
How many Units did the trainee have practice with student?	
How many units did the trainee role play?	

SCORE ON EDY QUIZ (PRE TEST)	
SCORE ON EDY QUIZ (POST TEST)	

TAF SCORE UNIT 8

Prepares Teaching =   Prompts =

Presents Task   =   Rewards =   **AVERAGE**

INSTRUCTORS NAME (Please print) ....

In your opinion does this trainee merit a certificate?
Please state your reasons :

....

....

....

Signed (Instructor) ....   Date ....

This form, together with the EDY course summary sheet, should be sent to the Centre for Educational Guidance and Special Needs, University of Manchester, Oxford Road, Manchester, M13 9PL.
Please mark the envelope "EDY DATA".

CEGSN use only
PASS/FAIL
Cert. No.